THE REAL YOU

UNVEILING THE HIDDEN PERSON OF THE HEART

DAVID SHEARIN

Unless otherwise indicated, Scripture taken from the New King James Version ®.

Copyright © 1982 by Thomas Nelson, Inc. Used by permission.

King James Bible. Nashville, TN: Holman Bible, 1973. Print.

The Amplified Bible. Used by permission of Zondervan Publishing. All rights reserved.

The Twentieth Century New Testament ©1978 by Richard Frances Weymouth. Published by Kregel Publications, Grand Rapids, MI. Used by permission. All rights reserved.

The Translators New Testament, The British & Foreign Bible Society. London. All rights reserved.

Romans, Tyndale New Testament Commentaries, F.F. Bruce. Wm. B. Eerdmans Publishing Company, Grand Rapids, MI. Used by permission. All rights reserved.

Helen Barrett Montgomery, Centenary Translation of the New Testament. Public Domain

New Living Translation, copyright © 1996, 2004, 2007, 2013 by Tyndale House Foundation. Used by permission of Tyndale House Publishers, Inc., Carol Stream, Illinois 60188. All rights reserved. Used by permission

William Barclay, The New Testament Volume II, Published by Westminster John Knox Press. Used by permission of the publisher. All rights reserved.

Scripture quotations marked (TLB) are taken from *The Living Bible* copyright © 1971. Used by permission of Tyndale House Publishers, Inc., Wheaton, IL 60189. All rights reserved. Used by permission

Letters to Young Churches, J.B. Phillips. Simon and Schuster. Used by permission. All rights reserved.

Scripture taken from the HOLY BIBLE, NEW INTERNATIONAL VERSION ®, NIV ®. Copyright © 1973, 1978, 1984 by International Bible Society. Used by permission of Zondervan Publishing House. All rights reserved.

Scripture taken from THE MESSAGE, copyright © 1993, 1994, 1995, 1996, 2000, 2001, 2002. Used by permission of NavPress Publishing Group.

Blackwelder, Boyce W. *Letters from Paul: An Exegetical Translaton.* Anderson, IN: Warner, 1971. Print. Used by permission

Vine, William E., and F. F. Bruce. *Vine's Expository Dictionary of Old and New Testament Words.* IA Falls, IA: World Bible, 1971. Print. Used by permission

Hagin, Kenneth E. *I Went to Hell.* Tulsa, OK: K. Hagin Ministries, 1982. Print. Used by permission

Penn-Lewis, Jessie. *"Soul and Spirit": A Glimpse into Bible Teaching on the Highway to Spiritual Maturity.* Leicester: "Overcomer" Office, 1913. Print. Used by permission

Jordan, Clarence. *The Cotton Patch Version of Paul's Epistles*. Piscataway, NJ: Association, 1982. Print. Used by permission

Strong, James. *Strong's Exhaustive Concordance of the Bible: With Greek and Hebrew Dictionary*. Nashville: Regal Pub, 1978. Print. Used by permission

The New American Bible. New York, NY: Oxford UP, 2004. Print. Used by permission

Rotherham, Joseph Bryant. *The Emphasized Bible, a New Translation* .. Cincinnati: Standard Pub., 1902. Print. Used by permission

Wade, G. W. *The Documents of the New Testament: Translated & Historically Arranged, with Critical Introductions*. Place of Publication Not Identified: Publisher Not Identified, 1982. Print. Used by permission

Bruce, F. F. *The Letters of Paul: An Expanded Para-phrase Printed in Parallel with the Revised Version* ... Grand Rapids: Eerdmans, 1965. N. pag. Print. Used by permission

Wuest, Kenneth Samuel. *The New Testament; an Expanded Translation*. Grand Rapids: Eerdmans, 1988. Print. Used by permission

New American Standard Bible. Nashville: T. Nelson, 1979. Print. Used by permission

Sparks, T. Austin. *What Is Man?* Tulsa, OK: Emmanuel Church, 1939. Print.

Bosworth, F. F. *Christ the Healer*. Place of Publication Not Identified: Bottom Of The Hill Publis, 2011. Print.

Webster's Dictionary. Nashville: Thomas Nelson, 1991. Print.

Hamblen, Stuart. "This Ole House." Ain't a-gonna need this house no longer, ain't a gonna need this house no more, Ain't got time to fix the shingles, ain't got time to fix the floor, Ain't got time to oil the hinges or to mend the window pane, Ain't a gonna need this house no longer, I'm getting ready to meet the saints. This Ole House. 1954.

SHEARIN, DAVID. *MASTER KEY*. S.l.: WINTERS GROUP, 2015. Print.

The Real You
Unveiling the Hidden Person of the Heart
ISBN 978-1-940697-09-3
Copyright © 2017 by David Shearin

Published by
David Shearin Ministries
3520 N. Buffalo Dr.
Las Vegas, NV 89129
www.thewordforliving.com

Printed in the United States of America. All rights reserved under international Copyright Law. Contents and/or cover may not be reproduced in whole or in part in any form without the express written consent of the publisher.

CONTENTS

Introduction 7

Chapter 1: You Are God's Design 11

Chapter 2: Spirit, Soul and Body 19

Chapter 3: Possessing Your Soul 31

Chapter 4: Your Body, Your House 39

Chapter 5: Your Spirit is Eternal 51

Chapter 6: Distinguishing Between Soul and Spirit 61

Chapter 7: Becoming Spirit Conscious 71

Chapter 8: Renewing Your Mind 83

Chapter 9: Flesh vs. Spirit 95

Chapter 10: Serving God with Your Spirit 109

Scriptures 119

About the Author 142

Introduction

Did you know that your voice and the shape of your ears are just as unique as your fingerprints? You are no accident. You are God's creation, His unique design. The Bible says you are *"fearfully and wonderfully made."*[1] God not only created your body uniquely, He created your spirit and soul with potential for greatness you haven't even dreamed of!

Life has many obstacles and various challenges, as I'm sure you know. The circumstances of life oftentimes seem overwhelming and the disappointments crushing. My father died when I was eight years old. I received the shocking news of his death, not from my mother or a sibling, who might be able to comfort me, but from a neighbor as I was sitting on the steps of our home in "The Projects." I sat there alone and cried, without anyone to explain to me how or why my daddy died. I will never forget the pain I experienced that day.

I grew up in poverty, without a dad. When I became a teenager, I battled severe depression. Condemning and defeating thoughts bombarded my mind. I happened to have

---

[1] Psalm 139:14

relatives on both sides of my family who were in mental institutions and at one point; I thought I too was going to lose my mind. The devil painted a very bleak picture of me in the same depressed and defeated condition as some of my relatives.

I had become a Christian and I truly loved God, but the devil was trying his best to stop God's plan for my life. I'm so thankful for the prayers of my pastors, my mother and others. I believe the help and revelation that I received, and that I'm sharing with you in this book, came to me as a result of their prayers.

Victory in my life began when the Holy Spirit revealed to me that I was a spirit. I began to understand that the negative thoughts coming to my mind were not "me." As a teenager I was reading my Bible one day, and I suddenly got a revelation of Hebrews 4:12: "For the Word of God is living and powerful, and sharper than any two-edged sword, piercing even to the division of soul and spirit, and of joints and marrow, and is a discerner of the thoughts and intents of the heart." I suddenly understood that there was a distinct difference between my spirit (the real me) and my soul (my mind, will and emotions). From that point, I knew that I could choose which thoughts to think. I will never forget the joy I experienced that day! Gaining an understanding of spirit, soul and body set me free, changed my life, and set me on the course God had planned for me.

I also began to discover who I was in Christ, which

"unlocked" the New Testament for me.[2] I'm writing this book because I believe God has a wonderful purpose for your life and He wants you to discover it and live it. He desires for you to experience a fulfilling, satisfying, and abundant life. He created you to be victorious! The insights I share in the following chapters helped me overcome my fears, insecurities, disappointments and even demonic oppression. I am confident that you too can overcome any obstacles life may have thrown in your way when you discover… **the real you!**

---

[2] See my book, ***The Master Key***

CHAPTER 1

YOU ARE GOD'S DESIGN

Then God said, "Let Us make man in Our image, according to Our likeness; let them have dominion over the fish of the sea, over the birds of the air, and over the cattle, over all the earth and over every creeping thing that creeps on the earth." So God created man in His own image; in the image of God He created him; male and female He created them. Then God blessed them, and God said to them, "Be fruitful and multiply; fill the earth and subdue it; have dominion over the fish of the sea, over the birds of the air, and over every living thing that moves on the earth." (Genesis 1:26-28)

God is the Designer and Creator of mankind. In the first chapter of the book of Genesis we discover that God created three classes of life: plant life, animal life and human life. God didn't say, Let Us make the trees in Our image. Nor did He say, Let Us make animals in Our image. God said, "Let Us make man in Our image." The next verse says…"male

THE REAL YOU

and female He created them." So, when the Bible uses the term "man," generally speaking, it refers to "mankind" (both male and female).

Plants don't have bodies or souls, but they are a form (or class) of life. Animals have bodies and souls (intellectual and emotional qualities); yet they are another class of life. What is it that sets man apart from plants and animals? The answer is, man is a spirit, created in the image and likeness of God.

The Hebrew word translated God in Genesis 1:26-28 is Elohiym, which is actually the plural name for God. The Amplified Bible says, *"Let Us [Father, Son, and Holy Spirit] make mankind in Our image..."* The scriptures reveal that God is a Trinity: Father, Son and Holy Spirit. The Father, Son and Holy Spirit were all at work in creation. God said, *"Let Us make man in Our image."* Since God created man in His own image, man must also be a triune being. Man was created as spirit, soul and body.[3]

God Forms Man's Body

"The time came when the Lord God formed a man's body from the dust of the ground and breathed into it the breath of life. And man became a living person." (Genesis 2:7 TLB)

Before God created man, a mist came up from the face of the earth and watered the ground.[4] This mist made the dust of the earth into pliable clay for God to form man's body. Like a potter creating a vessel, God formed man's body.

[3] I Thessalonians 5:23
[4] Genesis 2:6

In the book of Job, the oldest book in the Bible, Elihu says to Job, *"I am the same as you in God's sight; I too am a piece of clay."* (Job 33:6 NIV) The prophet Isaiah speaks of God and man in the same manner: *"But now, O LORD, You are our Father; We are the clay, and You our potter; And all we are the work of Your hand."* (Isaiah 64:8) Interestingly, science now confirms that the human body consists of the same basic material and chemical elements found in the soil of the earth.

After forming man from the dust of the earth, God breathed into Adam the breath of life. The Hebrew word translated breath is *ruach*, which also means spirit. *"Then the Lord God formed man from the dust of the ground and breathed into his nostrils the breath or spirit of life, and man became a living being."* (Genesis 2:7 AMP) Again we read in Job, *"The Spirit of God has made me, And the breath of the Almighty gives me life." (Job 33:4)* In the book of Numbers God is referred to as *"the God of the spirits of all flesh;"* (Numbers 27:16) Zechariah 12:1 says that God *"forms the spirit of man within him;"* in Ecclesiastes 12:7 we read, *"Then the dust will return to the earth as it was, And the spirit will return to God who gave it."* The Bible clearly teaches that the spirit of man came from the breath of God.

The substance of man's body came from the ground, but the substance of man's spirit came directly from God. God, who Himself is Spirit[5] and the Creator of the universe,

---

[5] John 4:24

breathed out of Himself into Adam. When God breathed the spirit of life into Adam's clay mold, he became a living being or a living soul. He arose to conscious life and received understanding. *"But there is a spirit in man, And the breath of the Almighty gives him understanding."* (Job 32:8)

Man did not evolve from plants or animals; he is the crown of God's creation. When it comes to the origin of man, evolution is a man-made theory that has never been conclusively or scientifically proven. The ape-man myth has missing links that have never been (and never will be) found. It actually takes more "faith" to believe that everything, including man, evolved out of nothing (or from chaos) than to accept the Biblical account of creation and God's design. If you dare to search the Scriptures with an open heart and mind, you will discover they hold the keys that unlock the mysteries of life.

God's Original Intent

Adam was created in God's image as a spirit being, possessing a soul and living in a body. His spirit was the dominating force. When Adam walked in the Garden of Eden, his spirit dominated his soul (his mind, will and emotions) and shone brightly through his earthly house of clay, his body. His body was luminous - clothed with light shining out from his spirit. Adam's body, equipped with five physical senses, enabled him to function in the material world God had created for him.

Adam's spirit was in union and fellowship with God. As God's son, he had the very life and nature of God in him. He also had a perfect mind and a perfect human body with which to function. Adam had the intellectual ability to name all the animals.[6] He was capable of thinking creatively. His mind was able to perfectly express his spirit. Adam and Eve possessed the spiritual and intellectual ability to rule the earth.

God gave Adam and Eve dominion over all creation.[7] This was God's original intent for man and is still His desire. He did not create man to be controlled by anything in this earth. His plan is for man to have dominion.

God created man because He desired fellowship. He did not create man as a puppet or a robot. He gave him a soul with a free will. Adam had the ability to choose to love and obey God or not to love and obey Him. God's desire was for Adam to choose to love Him out of his own volition.

The Fall of Man

If Adam had obeyed God's command, he would have remained in union and fellowship with God. He would have been allowed to partake of the tree of life in the midst of the garden, and his body would have lived forever. The body God created for him was not originally doomed to die.[8] Sadly, Adam chose to disobey. He had been allowed to

---

[6] Genesis 2:19-20
[7] Genesis 1:28
[8] Genesis 3:22-24

freely eat of every tree in the garden, but God commanded him not to eat of the tree of the knowledge of good and evil, and warned him that in the day he ate of it, he would surely die.[9] Adam's disobedience brought death and darkness to his spirit and mind, and mortality to his body. He lost his dominion. He began to be controlled from the outside rather than from his spirit on the inside.

Adam's sin has rightly been called "The Fall of Man" because man fell from his position of dominion and the order of his being was reversed from *spirit, soul and body* to *body, soul and spirit*. Adam sunk down into the vessel of his soul and began to let his natural reasoning, influenced by his physical senses, dominate him.

Adam and Eve immediately covered their nakedness and hid from the presence of God. They became afraid of God's presence because they had sinned and died spiritually. The Apostle Paul describes this condition of spiritual death in Ephesians 4:18: *"having their understanding darkened, being alienated from the life of God..."* Fear, confusion, loneliness, and disease are only a few of the consequences of sin entering into the human race. All of the sufferings of humanity can be traced back to Adam's sin and the tragic disruption of God's order and design.

"Therefore, as sin came into the world through one man, and death as the result of sin, so death spread to all men, [no one being able to stop it or to escape its power] because all men sinned." (Romans 5:12 AMP)

[9] Genesis 2:16-17

The Redemption of Man

As tragic and far reaching as "The Fall of Man" was, thankfully the redemption of man is far greater in its power and effects! "But even greater is God's wonderful grace and His gift of righteousness, for all who receive it will live in triumph over sin and death through this one man, Jesus Christ." (Romans 5:17 NLT)

Because of Christ's amazing work of redemption, we can be saved from the penalty and consequences of sin and live victoriously in every area of our lives. When you receive Jesus Christ as your Savior, God recreates you in Christ and uniquely designs you for His purpose. Ephesians 2:10 in the Amplified Bible says, "For we are God's [own] handiwork (His workmanship), recreated in Christ Jesus, [born anew] that we may do those good works which God predestined (planned beforehand) for us [taking paths which He prepared ahead of time], that we should walk in them [living the good life which He prearranged and made ready for us to live]."

Through union with Christ, you can live as a new creation controlled from within rather than from without by your circumstances. In the following chapters you will discover how God's order of **spirit, soul and body** can be restored in your experience. You will realize that you are a spirit, you have a soul, and you live in a body. Primarily you are a spirit. Your spirit is *the real you!*

THE REAL YOU

Confession

I am a spirit, I have a soul, and I live in a body. I don't have to allow my body or my soul to dictate how I live. Thank You Lord for recreating me in Christ Jesus, and for giving me a revelation of the real me.

Summary Questions

1. Why did God create man? What sets him apart from the plants and animals?

2. Describe the three parts of man. In what ways is man like God?

3. When and how did man become a "living being?"

4. Describe what happened to Adam and Eve after they disobeyed God. How did their sin affect the human race?

5. What did God do to redeem man back to Himself and restore his position of dominion?

CHAPTER 2
SPIRIT, SOUL AND BODY

"Now may the God of peace Himself sanctify you completely; and may your whole spirit, soul, and body be preserved blameless at the coming of our Lord Jesus Christ." (1Thessalonians 5:23)

The Apostle Paul, writing to the church in Thessalonica, expressed a prayer for the believers to be sanctified completely – spirit, soul and body. This verse of scripture clearly reveals that man is a triune being: **spirit, soul and body**. Man is not simply body and soul, two parts, as some have believed. There are three dimensions to man's being and there is a distinction between the spirit and the soul. Moreover, the order in which they are listed is significant. Paul did not say body, soul and spirit because that was not God's intent. The spirit is first and is to have the superiority.

Three Dimensions

Let's define these three dimensions of man's being:

THE REAL YOU

Spirit – (The Greek word translated spirit is *pneuma*.) The part of your being that is born again. Your spirit is the inward man that is not visible to your natural sight. The part of you that knows, connects with and understands God.

Soul – (The Greek word translated soul is *psuche*.) The mind, will, and emotional part of a person. The soul is the intermediate part that stands between your spirit and your body. The soul can relate to and be influenced by your flesh or by your spirit. Your soul has the power to choose if it will be controlled by the flesh or by the spirit.

Body – *(The Greek word translated body is **soma**.)* Your body relates with the physical world. It is the house in which we the spirit live. The body is for executing and transacting the business of the spirit through the soul.

In order to be effective living the Christian life, it is essential to have a clear understanding of this truth: ***You are a spirit, you have (possess) a soul, and you live in a body.*** Reading the New Testament without this revelation is like viewing a 3-D movie without the 3-D glasses. The 3-D effect is lost and you do not enjoy the film as intended. God wants to give you a pair of 3-D glasses – a clear understanding of spirit, soul and body - so you can get the most out of your study of the Bible and your Christian life!

Primarily, you are a spirit. This is what sets you apart from animals. God gave Adam and Eve dominion over the animal kingdom[10] because they were in a different

---
[10] Genesis 1:26-28

class and of a higher order than animals. God created man (male and female) in His own image. (As we established in chapter one, when the Bible speaks of "man," it is generally referring to "mankind." Women have been subjugated and oppressed in every culture as a result of "The Fall," but wherever Christianity has flourished women have been elevated and their dignity has been restored.)

God is a Spirit

In The Gospel of John, chapter four, we read about Jesus speaking with a woman of Samaria while she is drawing water from a well. Jesus asked her for a drink. The woman was surprised that He would speak with her because, number one, she was a woman, and secondly she was a Samaritan woman and the Jews had no dealings with Samaritans. Jesus, however, cared for this woman and told her she could drink water from Him and never thirst again. Of course He was not speaking of natural water, but of spiritual water. He explained that the water He gives is eternal life and it would reside like a well on the inside of her and satisfy her like nothing else in this physical world.

Jesus knew the woman was unsatisfied with her life. She had been married five times and was living with a man outside of marriage. Jesus offered her the satisfaction for which her heart (her spirit) was longing.

In the course of their conversation, the woman asked Jesus about the proper location for worship. (The Samaritans didn't worship in Jerusalem like the Jews). Notice Jesus'

THE REAL YOU

answer:

> *"Woman, believe Me, the hour is coming when you will neither on this mountain, nor in Jerusalem, worship the Father. You worship what you do not know; we know what we worship, for salvation is of the Jews. But the hour is coming, and now is, when the true worshipers will worship the Father in spirit and truth; for the Father is seeking such to worship Him. God is Spirit, and those who worship Him must worship in spirit and truth." (John 4:21-24)*

First, Jesus brings her attention from the location of worship to the object of worship – the Father. Then He explains that because **God is a Spirit**, our worship must be spiritual – originating from our spirit, not from our mind or body. The Amplified Bible (vs. 24) says, *"God is a Spirit (a spiritual Being) and those who worship Him must worship Him in spirit and in truth (reality)."*

God made man in His image; therefore, **man is a spirit**. God's primary purpose for creating man was fellowship. He created us as spirit beings, in the same class so-to-speak as Himself, so that we could have an intimate relationship with Him. Jesus said this is what the Father is seeking. This is also what the Samaritan woman was seeking. This is what every person is seeking. This is what Jesus came to give! He came to restore man's relationship and fellowship with God.

The Blackwelder translation of John 4:24 says, *"God in His essential nature is Spirit."* The fact that God is a Spirit does not mean He doesn't have shape or form. It doesn't mean He is a cloud or a vapor. On the contrary, the Scriptures reveal that God has a face[11] and body parts. He has eyes,[12] ears,[13] arms,[14] hands,[15] fingers,[16] and back parts.[17] He sits on a throne[18] and has a footstool for His feet![19] God created man in His image. The Hebrew word translated image is Tsehlem. It means resemblance. Man's body is simply the physical reflection of his spirit, which resembles God.

You Must Be Born Again

In the third chapter of the Gospel of John, we read about Jesus speaking to a religious leader named Nicodemus. Like the Samaritan woman, Nicodemus also had questions for Jesus so he came to Him privately one night. Jesus surprised him with this statement:

"Most assuredly, I say to you, unless one is born again, he cannot see the kingdom of God." (John 3:3)

Since Jesus coined the term "born again," Nicodemus had never before heard such an expression. He, being a grown man, wondered how Jesus could be telling him to be born

---

[11] Psalm 34:16
[12] Isaiah 1:15
[13] Isaiah 59:2
[14] Isaiah 62:8
[15] Isaiah 59:1
[16] Exodus 31:18, Psalm 8:3
[17] Exodus 33:23
[18] Revelation 4:2
[19] Psalm 99:5

THE REAL YOU

again. He was thinking naturally or physically. He said, "How can a man be born when he is old? Can he enter a second time into his mother's womb and be born?" (John 3:4) This is how Jesus replied:

"That which is born of the flesh is flesh, and that which is born of the Spirit is spirit. Do not marvel that I said to you, 'You must be born again.'" (John 3:6-7)

When Jesus said, **"*you*** must be born again," He was referring to **"*the real you,*"** the spirit. In essence, Jesus was saying," You, Nicodemus (not your body), ***you*** must be born again." Nicodemus was a ruler of the Jews. He was a member of the Sanhedrin, a very religious sect. Your religious affiliation or background doesn't matter, nor does your gender, nationality, or social status. Jesus said, "**You must be born again.**"

When I was a teenager, I met a girl who tried to convince me that Jesus was talking about reincarnation when he spoke of being born again. However, she apparently didn't read the passage carefully because Jesus explains Himself very clearly:

"Men can only reproduce human life, but the Holy Spirit gives new life from heaven; so don't be surprised at my statement that you must be born again!" (John 3:6-7 TLB)

In the next verse (v. 8) Jesus illustrates the work of the Holy Spirit in the new birth by comparing it to the wind:

"The wind blows where it wishes, and you hear the sound

of it, but cannot tell where it comes from and where it goes. So is everyone who is born of the Spirit." (John 3:8)

I live in Las Vegas, Nevada, a very windy city. When the wind blows you can see the palm trees swaying and the dust swirling. Dead, dry sage brush tumble across the roads just like you've seen in the old western movies. Sometimes you can also hear the wind whistling and howling as it blows between buildings. Someone might exclaim, "Look at the wind blow!" But in reality we cannot see the wind; we can only see and hear the effects of the wind blowing. So it is when a person is born again. We cannot see the Holy Spirit and we cannot see a person's spirit, but we can see the effects of the new birth.

The Bible calls the spirit *"the hidden person of the heart."*[20] When a person has been born again, his or her life begins to change from the inside, out. The new birth has an effect upon one's countenance, attitude and conduct. You can see a person's countenance light up. You can see a change in lifestyle. You can observe a believer walking in God's peace. But, like the wind, you cannot actually see the spirit.

God Sees the Heart

"rather let it be the hidden person of the heart, with the incorruptible beauty of a gentle and quiet spirit, which is very precious in the sight of God." (1 Peter 3:4)

---

[20] 1 Peter 3:4

THE REAL YOU

In the third chapter of 1 Peter, verses 1-4, the apostle Peter is exhorting wives whose husbands are not Christians. He tells them to adorn themselves with *"the hidden man of the heart."* (v.4) In other words, he tells the wives to "wear" what is on the inside of them so that it is evident on the outside. This passage of scripture promises that if a Christian wife will be respectful to her unbelieving or disobedient husband, displaying a *"gentle and quiet spirit,"* her husband will be won over without her preaching to him. What a powerful promise!

I think about my aunt whose husband became an alcoholic after his doctor prescribed drinking alcohol when he was in the Navy. As a kid, I remember several occasions witnessing my aunt laughing and rejoicing in the Lord in spite of my uncle's belligerent drunken behavior. Instead of reacting in anger or getting discouraged, she maintained a gentle and peaceful spirit. Eventually, my uncle was born again and quit drinking!

Peter calls the spirit *"the hidden person of the heart."* In the same verse he says that it is *"in the sight of God."* So even though the spirit is "hidden," God sees it.

If you are in a situation like the one Peter was addressing, do not become discouraged! For a while, your spouse may not notice the change that has happened on the inside of you, but be assured God sees everything! At first your unbelieving spouse may become "testy"- testing you to see what you're really made of. People want to know if being born again is real. But if you will patiently do what is right in the sight of God, eventually your spouse (or even your co-worker, friend, or other relative) will be convinced.

Another verse of scripture that speaks of God seeing the heart is found in the book of First Samuel. The prophet Samuel was instructed by God to go and anoint one of Jesse's sons to be Israel's king in the place of Saul. When he saw Eliab, he was sure this son of Jesse must be the one. But The Lord said to Samuel, *"Do not look at his appearance or at his physical stature, because I have refused him. For the Lord does not see as man sees; for man looks at the outward appearance, but the Lord looks at the heart."* (1 Samuel 16:7) God had been observing David's heart as he was tending to his father's sheep. He had a faithful heart. He also had a heart full of worship toward God. His father didn't even recognize his leadership potential. He was overlooked and not even considered a candidate. Yet he was God's choice.

In the New Testament, the Apostle Paul spoke of those *"who boast in appearance and not in heart."*[21] For the most part, the Bible uses the terms "heart" and "spirit" interchangeably. The heart that God sees, as referred to in these verses, is not the physical organ that pumps blood to the rest of the body. When we speak of "the heart of a tree" or "the heart of the matter," we mean the core of the tree or the central, most important part of the matter. Your spirit is your heart - the most important part of you.

[21] 2 Corinthians 5:12

THE REAL YOU

You Are a New Creation

In 2 Corinthians 5:16, Paul wrote, *"Therefore, from now on, we regard no one according to the flesh. Even though we have known Christ according to the flesh, yet now we know Him thus no longer."* We are to see others and ourselves after the spirit, not according to outward distinctions. We should look beyond people's present fleshly attitudes and tendencies and continue to believe in them (not make excuses for their behavior, but continue to believe in them) because of who they are in Christ. This begins by knowing Jesus, looking at Him and seeing ourselves in Him.

Next Paul said, *"Therefore, if anyone is in Christ, he is a new creation."* (v.17) When you are born again, you don't become a new creation physically; you became a new creation inwardly.

The first man, Adam, was created in the image and likeness of God. Jesus Christ came to restore what mankind lost through "The Fall." Through the new birth, the Holy Spirit recreates your spirit in the image and likeness of God.

In Ephesians 4:24, the Apostle Paul exhorts believers to "put on" this new creation: *"and that you put on the new man which was created according to God, in true righteousness and holiness."* The Amplified Bible says, *"And put on the new nature (the regenerate self) created in God's image, [Godlike] in true righteousness and holiness."*

Jesus, Peter and Paul all affirm that the real you is a spirit.

Jesus said in Matthew 18:16, *"by the mouth of two or three witnesses every word may be established."* When you are born again, your spirit is recreated in true righteousness and holiness. That's good news! <u>You</u> are a new creation because your spirit is **the real you!**

Confession

I am a new creation in Christ. I choose to live according to the spirit and not according to the dictates of the flesh. I am created in God's image in true righteousness and holiness. God, I thank You that You see my heart, the real me, and You are helping me change my behavior from the inside out.

Summary Questions

1. Why is the order of spirit, soul and body significant?

2. What is meant by the statement, "God wants to give you a pair of 3-D glasses?" (P.10)

3. How is the new birth compared to the wind?

4. Who sees "the hidden person of he heart?" Why is this important?

5. In Ephesians 4:24, what does Paul exhort believers to "put on?"

CHAPTER 3
POSSESSING YOUR SOUL

By your patience possess your souls. (Luke 21:19)

Your soul consists of your mind, your will and your emotions. You are not a soul. You are a spirit, you have (possess) a soul, and you live in a body. In Luke chapter 21 Jesus is speaking about the last days and the signs of His second coming. He warns His disciples that they will be persecuted for His name's sake. In verse 16 He says that some will even be betrayed by family members. Then He gives them instruction on how to endure being hated by people: *"By your patience possess your souls."* (v.19) This verse indicates that your soul is not "you." Jesus said you can and should possess your soul.

When you are persecuted, hated and betrayed by people, the emotional pain can put pressure on you to react in anger or retaliation but Jesus said you can possess your soul by patience, which is a fruit of the spirit according to Galatians 5:22. Patience is in your spirit. When you are in a situation that causes you to feel anxious, angry, hurt, or lonely, you don't have to be controlled by those emotions. You can get a grip on your mind and possess your emotions with the fruit of patience that is in your spirit. Remember, your spirit is to be the dominating force in your life.

Galatians 5:16 says, *"Walk in the Spirit and you will not fulfill the lust of the flesh."* Verses 22-23 say, *"But the fruit of the Spirit is love, joy, peace, longsuffering (patience), kindness, goodness, faithfulness, gentleness, self-control."*

One way to activate patience or any of the other nine fruits of the Spirit, and take control of your soul, is to speak God's word. Instead of saying, "I don't know what I'm going to do. I'm so afraid!" Say what 2 Timothy 1:7 says, *"God has not given me a spirit of fear, but of power, love and a sound mind!"* Instead of speaking evil of your persecutors, or those who hurt you, say, *"The love of God has been poured out in my heart by the Holy Spirit."* (Romans 5:5) Say, *"Perfect love casts out all fear."* (1 John 4:18) God's word is a powerful, God-given weapon for pulling down strongholds in our minds and casting down imaginations contrary to the knowledge of God.[22]

Soul Purification

Remember: you are a spirit, you have a soul and you live in a body. But primarily, you are a spirit. 1 Peter 1:23 speaks of the spirit: *"having been born again, not of corruptible seed but incorruptible, through the Word of God which lives and*

---

[22] 2 Corinthians 10:4-5

abides forever." In verse 7 of this chapter, we are told that when our faith is tested by fire, it will come through the fire just like precious gold. In verse 22, Peter speaks of the soul: *"Since you have purified your souls in obeying the truth through the Spirit..."* In verse 24 he speaks of the flesh: *"all flesh is as grass."* All three parts of man are represented in this passage: the spirit, which is incorruptible, the soul, which is purified through obedience, and the body, which is temporary and quickly withers like the grass.

When you're going through a difficult time, remind yourself of who you are. You are born of an incorruptible seed. You are going to make it through this trial! When your soul is purified through obedience to the truth, you are able to express your spirit and who you are in Christ more effectively. This will result in other people's lives being touched and changed.

After gold has been purified, it can be made into fine jewelry or used to make beautiful vessels. When our faith is tested and our souls are purified, we can live in a way that is useful to God and testifies to others that Jesus is alive! Isn't that what being a Christian is all about?

Rejoice!

Another way to ensure that your spirit maintains superiority is to rejoice even when you don't feel like it. James 1:2-4 says, *"My brethren, count it all joy when you fall into various trials, knowing that the testing of you faith produces patience. But let patience have its perfect work, that you may be perfect and complete, lacking nothing."* The Amplified Bible says, *"Consider it wholly joyful..."* When you're going through a trial, God's word says to consider it joyful. This is what my Aunt did when her husband came home drunk. You can always draw on the joy and the patience that is in your spirit. You can always rejoice "in the Lord!"[23]

The Apostle Peter said,

> *"Beloved, do not think it strange concerning the fiery trial which is to try you, as though some strange thing happened to you; but rejoice to the extent that you partake of Christ's sufferings, that when His glory is revealed, you may also be glad with exceeding joy. If you are reproached for the name of Christ, blessed are you, for the Spirit of glory and of God rests upon you." (1 Peter 4:12-14)*

Here again we are told to rejoice! In the last verse of this chapter (v.19) Peter says, *"Therefore let those who suffer according to the will of God* **commit their souls** *to Him in doing good, as to a faithful Creator."*

We can choose what to do with our soul when we are mistreated. The natural tendency is to defend ourselves or to take matters into our own hands. Instead, we must commit our soul to God and trust Him to vindicate us, while we continue to do the right thing. This isn't always easy but the reward is great! In this passage Peter said that the Spirit of glory and of God will rest upon us. In Matthew

---

[23] Philippians 4:4

Possessing Your Soul

5:11-12 Jesus said, *"Blessed are you when they revile and persecute you, and say all kinds of evil against you falsely for My sake. Rejoice and be exceedingly glad, for great is your reward in heaven, for so they persecuted the prophets who were before you."*

Let's consider what Paul and Silas did while they were in the Philippian jail. In Acts chapter 16 we read about how they were beaten with rods and imprisoned for preaching the gospel. Their feet were in stocks and their backs were bleeding. They were locked up in the innermost prison. This would be what prisoners today call "the hole!" It was dark. Do you think they *felt* like praising God? Silas could have said, "Paul, if I get out of here alive, this is the last missionary journey I'm taking with you!" Both of them could have complained or blamed each other. Instead, at midnight they prayed and sang praises to God![24] And they weren't quiet about it. It says the prisoners heard them. Suddenly an earthquake shook the foundation of the prison and all the prison doors were opened and everyone's chains were loosed. God did more than preserve the souls of Paul and Silas when they rejoiced; He brought the jailor to his knees and saved his entire household.

When Paul prayed for the church at Ephesus, he prayed that God would strengthen them with might through His spirit in their inner man.[25] He ended the prayer[26] by saying, "Now to

---

[24] Acts 16:25
[25] Ephesians 3:16
[26] Ephesians 3:20

THE REAL YOU

Him who is able to do exceeding abundantly above all that we ask or think, according to the power that works in us." When we choose to pray, speak God's Word, and rejoice no matter what we face or how we feel, God will show up and show out in ways we don't even expect!

Learn to rejoice in the middle of your trial and in the middle of your difficulty! Expect God to move on your behalf. Expect a victorious end. Keep your focus on God and His word. God promises to keep you in perfect peace when your mind is stayed on Him.[27] He also promises to hold your soul in life and not allow your foot to be moved.[28] You can do all things through Christ who strengthens you.[29] You do not have to be controlled by your emotions or your circumstances, even if you have been in the habit of living that way. You can begin now to possess your soul because of who you are in Christ. Remember: you are a spirit, you possess a soul, and you live in a body. Your spirit is *the real you!*

Confession

Thank you Lord that I am able to walk in all the fruits of the spirit and grow daily in each of them. I activate the fruit of the spirit in my life by speaking God's word. I rejoice when I don't feel like it - and I possess my soul because of who I am in Christ.

---

[27] Isaiah 26:3
[28] Psalm 66:9
[29] Philippians 4:13

Summary Questions

1. What does "possess your soul" mean and how can we do this, even when mistreated?

2. What is the fruit of the spirit according to Galatians 5:22?

3. According to 1 Peter 1:22, how is your soul "purified?"

4. Can you think of a time when you chose to rejoice when you didn't feel like it? What happened as a result?

5. The testing of your faith is compared to what? Explain this comparison.

CHAPTER 4
YOUR BODY, YOUR HOUSE

For we know that if our earthly house, this tent, is destroyed, we have a building from God, a house not made with hands, eternal in the heavens. (2 Corinthians 5:1)

Your body is simply the house in which you live. It is a temporary dwelling place according to the scriptures. If you are a Christian, you will get a new house one day.

Because the Holy Spirit dwells in you, your body is also the house of the Holy Spirit according to 1 Corinthians 6:19; *"Or do you not know that your body is the temple of the Holy Spirit who is in you, whom you have from God, and you are not your own?"* Verse 20 says, *"For you were bought at a price; therefore glorify God in your body and in your spirit, which are God's."*

We should take care of our body; most importantly, we should glorify God in our body because it really belongs

THE REAL YOU

to Him. He paid a high price for our entire being - spirit, soul and body. So, it is reasonable that we should present our bodies to Him as Paul said in Romans 12:1, *"I beseech you therefore, brethren, by the mercies of God, that you present your bodies a living sacrifice, holy, acceptable to God, which is your reasonable service."*

Your Body is Mortal

One of the most important things to understand about the body you have now is that it is mortal, meaning it is death-doomed. This is not particularly good news and there are many people over the centuries who have tried to find the "fountain of youth" to get rid of this mortality, but they have never found it. Others these days are trying to stretch, nip and tuck their bodies, but nothing can change this fact: Because of Adam's sin, our bodies are decaying and will eventually die unless Jesus comes back in our lifetime.

2 Corinthians 4:16-18 says,

> *"Therefore we do not lose heart. Even though our outward man is perishing, yet the inward man is being renewed day by day. For our light affliction, which is but for a moment, is working for us a far more exceeding and eternal weight of glory, while we do not look at the things, which are seen, but at the things which are not seen. For the things which are seen are temporary, but the things which are not seen are eternal."*

Verse 16 of this passage says, *"the outward man is perishing."* The Amplified Bible says, *"our outward man is [progressively] decaying and wasting away."* The only hope we have to overcome mortality is to receive eternal life through Jesus Christ. *"For God so loved the world that He gave His only begotten Son, that whoever believes in Him should not perish but have everlasting life." (John 3:16)*

Receiving a New Body

God promises to give us a new body at Christ's return. In verse 2 of 2 Corinthians 5, it says that we groan within ourselves, earnestly desiring to be clothed with our new, heavenly house. Verses 6-8 say, *"knowing that while we are at home in the body we are absent from the Lord. For we walk by faith, not by sight. We are confident, yes, well pleased rather to be absent from the body and to be present with the Lord."* So even if we go the way of the grave, dying before Jesus comes, our spirit will immediately go to be with the Lord.

Romans 8:23 also says we are groaning within ourselves, eagerly waiting for the redemption of our body. It was not God's original intent for our body to be mortal. Death is unnatural and that is why people fight it so vigorously. Death is called the "last enemy."[30]

God created Adam's body to live forever and if he had not sinned our bodies would not be death-doomed. So for

---

[30] 1 Corinthians 15:26

those of us who have eternal life on the inside of us, we are longing for the day when we will be free from this earth-bound, decaying body. Thank God, we will be free! We will receive a new body, fashioned like Jesus' glorious body.[31] W. E. Vine's, Greek definition for "eternal life," says, *"One day it (eternal life) will extend its domain to the sphere of our body."*

This is how it will happen:

> *"Behold, I tell you a mystery: We shall not all sleep (die), but we shall all be changed-in a moment, in the twinkling of an eye, at the last trumpet. For the trumpet will sound, and the dead will be raised incorruptible, and we shall be changed. For this corruptible must put on incorruption, and this mortal must put on immortality. So when this corruptible has put on incorruption, and this mortal has put on immortality, then shall be brought to pass the saying that is written: 'Death is swallowed up in victory.'"* (1 Corinthians 15:51-56)

Leaving the Body

My mother went home to be with the Lord at age 93. She had been born again and filled with the Holy Spirit since age 14 and never wavered in her devotion to the Lord. She went through many difficult times in her life. My dad died when she was in her forties and she never remarried. She went to work in a pillow factory to support the four children still at

---

[31] Philippians 3:21

home. She also buried three of her children (my siblings) during her lifetime. One of them was a baby. However, she was always praying, rejoicing, serving the Lord with gladness and always witnessing to people and helping people. She was a wonderful mother and a tremendous example of a Christian. She used to say to me, "I've made up my mind: I'm gonna be happy!" She lived for a purpose greater than herself and truly she is rejoicing now in heaven where she is fully herself enjoying her reward.

When Momma went to heaven, many of her children and grandchildren, including our daughter Ashley, were by her bedside. My wife, Vicki, and I were actually on vacation, riding a motorcycle in the Smoky Mountains of Tennessee when I received a call from my brother, Tony. Mark and Trina Hankins were with us, and that evening, in the cabin we were staying in, we got on speaker phone with my momma and other family members and Trina led us all in singing songs and hymns about heaven. I encouraged Momma that it was okay to let go and go home to be with Jesus. After a couple of hours of singing and rejoicing, she left her body and went to heaven. Actually Mark Hankins's mom, Velma, went home to be with the Lord the same way a few years before, with her family singing by her bedside.

Heaven is real! Although we had to bury my mother's body, we know that one day she will get a new body. In fact, one of the songs we sang that night was a fun old song Momma enjoyed singing in her later years especially. It was called, "This Old House." Here are the words to the chorus:

THE REAL YOU

"This Old House" by Stuart Hamblen

> *Ain't a-gonna need this house no longer, ain't a-gonna need this house no more,*
>
> *Ain't got time to fix the shingles, ain't got time to fix the floor,*
>
> *Ain't got time to oil the hinges or to mend the windowpane,*
>
> *Ain't a gonna need this house no longer, I'm getting ready to meet the saints.*

I believe we should take care of our bodies the best we can for as long as we can, and my mother did that. Her body was relatively healthy all her life. She rarely complained even of aches and pains in her old age. She would pray and confess healing scriptures. But no matter how well you take care of your body, it will decay and perish. We cannot change that fact. But we can look forward to Christ's return when we will see our loved ones again and we will all receive new bodies.

Christ's coming for His own is also described in 1 Thessalonians 4:15-18:

> *For this we say to you by the word of the Lord, that we who are alive and remain until the coming of the Lord will by no means precede those who are asleep. For the Lord Himself will descend from heaven with a shout, with the voice of an archangel, and with the*

trumpet of God. And the dead in Christ will rise first. Then we who are alive and remain shall be caught up together with them in the clouds to meet the Lord in the air. And thus we shall always be with the Lord. Therefore comfort one another with these words.

When the Apostle Paul was near the end of his life, he said he was hard-pressed between two choices, having on the one hand a desire to depart and be with Christ, which he said was "far better," and on the other hand he said to remain in the flesh was more needful for the church to which he was writing the letter.[32] He said the choice was actually up to him as to whether he would continue to live in his body or depart from his body and be with the Lord. He chose to stay a while longer in order to further minister to the church. But notice the language he used: depart or remain. He indicated that he was the same person whether in or out of the body.

In fact, in 2 Corinthians chapter 12, Paul talks about a powerful spiritual experience he had, some of which he said was not lawful for him to even talk about. When he wrote about this vision, or revelation, he said, "I know a man in Christ who fourteen years ago-whether in the body I do not know, or whether out of the body I do not know, God knows-how he was caught up into Paradise." (vv.2-4) Most Bible scholars agree that Paul was speaking of himself here, and I also agree with that interpretation. Paul could not even tell if he was in his body or out of his body because the body is not the man, it is only the "earth suit"

[32] Philippians 1:22-24

we wear to live here on earth.

You wouldn't go to the moon wearing a pair of shorts and a pair of flip-flops. You would need a "moon-suit" so that you could adapt to outer space. Astronauts wear specially designed suits to function when travelling outside the earth's atmosphere. Our bodies allow us to function in this earth realm, but we are eternal spirit beings who exist whether we are in our body or out of our body.

W.E.Vine, in his Expository Dictionary of New Testament Words, in the definition for soma (the Greek word translated body) said, " The body is not the man for he himself can exist apart from the body." The body cannot exist without the spirit ("The body without the spirit is dead." James 2:26), but the spirit, which is the real you, does exist apart from the body.

Dr. Richard Eby was a physician who fell off of a balcony and hit his head on the concrete. He cracked his skull and was pronounced clinically dead, but he miraculously recovered. He had an out-of-body experience, which he wrote about in his book, "A Physician's Account of Being Caught Up Into Paradise." This is how he described himself in heaven: "I looked like me, felt like me, reacted like me. I was me. I simply suddenly had shed the old body and was now living anew in this fantastic cloud-like body."

In James 1:10-11, our physical body is described as "a flower of the field" that will quickly pass away,[33] and our

---

[33] James 1:9

life here on earth is described in verse 14 as "a vapor that appears for a little time and then vanishes away."[34]

Toward the end of his life, the Apostle Peter, writing to the church, spoke in a very similar manner as the Apostle Paul regarding what his final purpose was before departing from his body:

> *For this reason I will not be negligent to remind you always of these things, though you know and are established in the present truth. Yes, I think it is right, as long as I am in this tent, to stir you up by reminding you, knowing that shortly I must put off my tent, just as our Lord Jesus Christ showed me. Moreover I will be careful to ensure that you always have a reminder of these things after my decease. (2 Peter 1:12-15)*

To Peter, dying was as simple as taking off a coat. Like Paul, when he used the pronoun "I" he was referring to his spirit. The Amplified Bible for verse 14 says, *"Since I know that the laying aside of this body of mine will come speedily, as our Lord Jesus Christ made clear to me."* And again, like Paul, he wanted to use the time he had remaining in his body to stir up the believers and remind them of the truth.

My spiritual father, Kenneth E. Hagin, went home to be with the Lord at age 86. He had said many times, "If you hear I'm gone, you'll know I was satisfied!" He said that based on Psalm 91:16, *"With long life I will satisfy him, And*

---

[34] James 4:14

show him My salvation." He taught the Bible in seminars, which sometimes lasted two weeks, with morning and evening meetings; right up to the time he went to heaven. It takes a lot out of you physically to do that even if you're a young man. But Dad Hagin, like Paul and Peter, wanted to stir up the church and put them in remembrance of things they may have already heard him say but needed to hear again. I'm so glad he did and I'm so glad I was in many of those meetings.

Controlling the Body

In 1 Corinthians 9:27 Paul said this: *"But I discipline my body and bring it into subjection, lest, when I have preached to others, I myself should become disqualified."* Even the Apostle Paul had to discipline his body. No one is going to do this for you. The Holy Spirit will help you, but He will not do it for you. Notice the language again in this verse. Paul said "I" bring "my body" into subjection. Who is "I?" Paul was referring to his spirit. He recognized that he could be disqualified in the race God had for him to run if he did not bring his body into subjection to his spirit. In this passage, he is exhorting believers to run their race, disciplining their bodies like an athlete who wants to win. He said they do it for a perishable crown, but we for an imperishable crown. (v. 25) It is unfortunate that so many Christians and even preachers have become disqualified as a result of not keeping their bodies under control. It's important for all of us to maintain a sober mind and humble attitude so we may stay in the race to receive our crown!

Until Jesus returns, or until we leave our body to be with the Lord, we are given specific instructions regarding what we are to do with our body. We are to present it to God as a living sacrifice.[35] We are to yield the members of our body to God as "instruments of righteousness."[36] We are to discipline our body and bring it into subjection to our spirit.[37] We need our body to finish the course God has for us on this earth; therefore, we should do our best to take care of it so we can live long and stay strong. Finally, one day we will all stand before the judgment seat of Christ to be rewarded for the things done in our body.[38]

Making the following confession regularly will help you become more spirit-conscious and help you finish your God-given race.

Confession

The spirit is who I am. The soul is what I possess. The body is where I live. I present my body to God as a living sacrifice. I yield my body to God as an instrument of righteousness. I bring my body under subjection to my spirit (the real me). I live with expectant hope of Jesus return when I will receive a new body like Jesus' glorified body.

---

[35] Romans 12:1
[36] Romans 6:13
[37] 1 Corinthians 9:27
[38] 2 Corinthians 5:10

THE REAL YOU

Summary Questions

1. Your body is simply the _____ in which you live.

2. God promises to give us a new body one day. Describe this glorious event.

3. Can your spirit (the real you) exist without your body? Explain.

4. According to Romans 12:1, what should we be doing with our bodies now?

CHAPTER 5

YOUR SPIRIT IS ETERNAL

"...the body without the spirit is dead." (James 2:26)

Your body is simply an "earth suit." It is temporary and mortal. Your spirit, on the other hand, is eternal. When you die, your spirit and soul will leave your body. Your body, which is composed of earthly elements, will return to the earth. According to the Bible, because all spirits are eternal, everyone will go to either heaven or hell when they die. As my spiritual father, renowned author and Bible teacher, Kenneth E. Hagin, so often said, *"There is a heaven to gain and a hell to shun!"* He knew this not only from reading the Bible but also from his own personal experience.

"I Went to Hell"

In his mini-book, "I Went to Hell" Brother Hagin describes what it was like to leave his body before he was born again. His mother was out on the porch praying for him at the top of her lungs when God intervened, rescuing him from

THE REAL YOU

the gates of hell. His testimony is fascinating and riveting. After God saved him and raised him up from a deathbed, he began preaching at school and on street corners at age 17. He got people's attention and drew a crowd by saying, *"I'd know there was a hell if I didn't have a Bible!"* He continued to preach the gospel for nearly 70 years before he left his body and went to heaven. Notice in his account how he was no less himself whether he was in his body or out of his body:[39]

> *Just as Grandpa's clock struck 7:30, my heart stopped beating within my bosom. And I could feel, faster than you could snap your fingers, the blood cease to circulate way down at the end of my toes. My toes seemed to go numb. This numbness spread to my feet, my ankles, my knees, my hips, my stomach, my heart - and I leaped out of my body... like a diver would leap off of a diving board into a swimming pool. I knew I was outside of my body. I could see my family in the room, but I couldn't contact them. I had it in my mind to say goodbye to Momma, Granny, and my little brother, but I leaped out of my body before I could get the words out fully. I began to descend - down, down, into a pit, like you'd go down into a well, cavern, or cave. I did not know that my physical voice picked that up. As I was trying to say goodbye, I knew I was going down into that place. All three of my family members who were present testified later, "When you said goodbye, your voice*

---

[39] "I Went to Hell" by Kenneth E Hagin

Your Spirit is Eternal

sounded like you were way down in a cave or cavern or something." And I continued to descend. I went down feet first - down, down, down, down. I could look up and see the lights of the earth. They finally faded away. Darkness encompassed me 'round about – darkness that is blacker than any night man has ever seen. It seemed that if you had a knife, you could cut a chunk of it out. You couldn't see your hand if it was one inch in front of your nose. The farther down I went, the darker it became - and the hotter it became - until finally, way down beneath me, I could see fingers of light playing on the wall of darkness. And I came to the bottom of the pit. This happened to me more than 60 years ago, yet it's just as real to me as if it had happened week before last. Spiritual things never grow old. When I came to the bottom of the pit, I saw what caused the fingers of light to play on the wall of darkness. Out in front of me, beyond the gates or the entrance into hell, I saw giant, great orange flames with a white crest. I was pulled toward hell just like a magnet pulls metal unto itself. I knew that once I entered through those gates, I could not come back. I endeavored to slow down my descent, because when I came to the bottom of the pit, there still was a slant downward. I was conscious of the fact that some kind of a creature met me at the bottom of that pit. I didn't look at it. My gaze was riveted on the gates, yet I knew that a creature was there by my right side. I didn't know

THE REAL YOU

until a good many years later, when I discovered it in the Book of Isaiah, that the Bible says, "Hell from beneath is moved for thee to meet thee at thy coming: it stirreth up the dead for thee...." (Isaiah 14:9). That creature, when I endeavored to slow down my descent, took me by the arm to escort me in. When he did, away above the blackness and the darkness a voice spoke. It sounded like a male voice, but I don't know what he said. I don't know whether it was God, Jesus, an angel, or who. He did not speak in the English language; it was a foreign language. That place just shook at the few words he spoke! And the creature took his hand off of my arm. There was a power like a suction to my back parts that pulled me back. I floated away from the entrance to hell until I stood in the shadows. Then, like a suction from above, I floated up, headfirst, through the darkness. Before I got to the top, I could see the light. I've been down in a well; it was like you were 'way down in a well and could see the light up above. I came up on the porch of my Grandpa's house. We lived in one of those old fashioned houses they used to build down in Texas with a porch nearly all the way around the house. I came up on the south side of the house. I could see Grandpa's porch swing there. I could see the giant cedar trees in the yard. I stood there on the porch just for a second. Then I went right through the wall - not through the door, and not through the window - through the wall, and seemed to leap inside my body like a man would slip his foot inside his boot in the morning time. Before I leaped inside my body, I could see my grandmother sitting on the edge of the bed holding me in her arms. When I got inside of my body, I could communicate with her.

Did you notice that Brother Hagin described his near-death experience as "leaping out of his body?" When he returned from "the gates of hell" he said, "I seemed to leap inside my body like a man would slip his foot inside his boot in the morning time." His description of leaping in and out of his body underscores the scriptural truth that your spirit is the real you and your body merely an earth suit.

All Spirits Are Eternal

In W. E. Vine's Expository Dictionary of New Testament Words, included in the definition of body (Greek, soma), it says, *"The body is not the man for he himself can exist apart from his body."*

All spirit beings are eternal. God is a Spirit[40] and He is eternal. Angels are spirits and they are eternal. Demons are spirits and they are eternal. Man is a spirit, so man is eternal. The question is, where will you spend eternity when you leave your body? Jesus said, *"Most assuredly, I say to you, unless one is born again, he cannot see the kingdom of God."* (John 3:3)

The Rich Man and Lazarus

In Luke 16:19-31 Jesus tells of a certain rich man who died.

---
[40] John 4:4

THE REAL YOU

Bible Scholars agree that this was a true story and not just a parable because of the unique terminology He uses to describe the characters and the story:

> *There was a certain rich man who was clothed in purple and fine linen and fared sumptuously every day. But there was a certain beggar named Lazarus, full of sores, who was laid at his gate, desiring to be fed with the crumbs, which fell from the rich man's table. Moreover the dogs came and licked his sores. So it was that the beggar died, and was carried by the angels to Abraham's bosom. The rich man also died and was buried. And being in torments in Hades, he lifted up his eyes and saw Abraham afar off, and Lazarus in his bosom. "Then he cried and said, 'Father Abraham, have mercy on me, and send Lazarus that he may dip the tip of his finger in water and cool my tongue; for I am tormented in this flame.' But Abraham said, 'Son, remember that in your lifetime you received your good things, and likewise Lazarus evil things; but now he is comforted and you are tormented. And besides all this, between us and you there is a great gulf fixed, so that those who want to pass from here to you cannot, nor can those from there pass to us.' "Then he said, 'I beg you therefore, father, that you would send him to my father's house, for I have five brothers, that he may testify to them, lest they also come to this place of torment.' Abraham said to him, 'They have Moses*

and the prophets; let them hear them.' And he said, 'No, father Abraham; but if one goes to them from the dead, they will repent.' But he said to him, 'If they do not hear Moses and the prophets, neither will they be persuaded though one rise from the dead.'

Lazarus and the rich man both died and their spirits left their bodies. Lazarus went to Abraham's bosom, a place of comfort. (Before Jesus' death and resurrection, the righteous who died went to this place. Now, heaven is the destination for those who are born again). When the rich man died, his body was buried but he found himself in Hades (Hell), a place of torment.

Even though the rich man had left his body, he still had eyes; he saw father Abraham. He also had a tongue and the sensation of torment from the flames of hell. Again, we see from the story that man is a spirit, possessing a soul. The soul contains our memories and goes with our spirit when we die. The rich man recognized Lazarus and remembered how, in his lifetime, Lazarus suffered as a beggar while he "fared sumptuously."

Inward Man vs. Outward Man

In Paul's second letter to the Corinthians, he wrote about the inward man and the outward man: *"Even though our outward man is perishing, yet the inward man is being renewed day by day." (2 Corinthians 4:16)* Then he said, *"For we know that if our earthly house, this tent, is destroyed, we have a building from God, a house not made with hands, eternal*

THE REAL YOU

in the heavens." (2 Corinthians 5:1) Paul referred to the body as the "outward man" and to the spirit as the "inward man." The outward man is mortal or "perishing." He also called the body a "tent" - a fragile, temporary dwelling. He explained that if the tent is destroyed (that is, if we die before Jesus returns) our spirit will move to a permanent, eternal home - *"a building from God, not made with human hands, but an eternal home in the heavens made with God's hands."* Finally, he wrote:

> *So we are always confident, knowing that while we are at home in the body we are absent from the Lord. For we walk by faith, not by sight. We are confident, yes, well pleased rather to be absent from the body and to be present with the Lord. (2 Corinthians 5:6-8)*

In chapter 4 we pointed out that the Apostle Paul expressed a struggle in deciding whether or not he would stay in his body for a while longer or *"depart and be with Christ."* He indicated that this was his choice. He said to depart and be with Christ "is far better," but to stay in the flesh would be more needful for the disciples to whom he was ministering. Paul was clearly conscious that he was a spirit being, simply using his body to carry out God's purposes while on the earth. Similarly, Peter wrote, *"Yes, I think it is right, as long as I am in this tent, to stir you up by reminding you, knowing that shortly I must put off my tent, just as our Lord Jesus Christ showed me."* (2 Peter 1:13-14)

To Paul and Peter, putting off the body was as simple as

taking off an article of clothing. At the moment of death, a believer's spirit slips out of the body and enters heaven; an unbeliever's spirit slips out of the body and descends into hell. This is because the spirit is eternal.

You are a spirit, you have a soul and you live in a body. But primarily you are a spirit. Your spirit is *the real you*.

Confession

Thank you, God, for sending your Son, Jesus Christ to die for my sins so that I could be saved and go to heaven when I die! I believe you raised Jesus from the dead and I confess Him as my Lord. My spirit is born again. Although my "outward man" is perishing, my "inward man" – my spirit - the real me - is renewed day by day.

Summary Questions

1. What happens to a person's spirit and soul when he or she dies?

2. According to 2 Corinthians 4:16, what is happening daily to our "outward man?" What about our "inward man?"

3. I am a _____, I have a _____ and I live in a _____.

4. Kenneth E. Hagin used to say this about eternity, "There is a _____ to gain, and a _____ to shun!"

CHAPTER 6

DISTINGUISHING BETWEEN SOUL AND SPIRIT

For the word of God is living and powerful, and sharper than any two-edged sword, piercing even to the division of soul and spirit, and of joints and marrow, and is a discerner of the thoughts and intents of the heart. (Hebrews 4:12)

When I was a teenager, the Holy Spirit used the above scripture to dramatically change my life. I had been born again and I loved God, but the devil attacked my mind. I was bombarded with negative, condemning thoughts. Even when I would try to read my Bible, the devil would twist the scriptures and use them to condemn me. Have you ever experienced that? My Father died when I was eight years old, and I didn't feel like I had anyone to talk to. The devil tried to destroy my mind and stop me from fulfilling the call of God upon my life. Thank God, I came upon this verse of scripture (Hebrews 4:12), and the Holy Spirit opened my eyes and set me free!

THE REAL YOU

I saw, while reading Hebrews 4:12, that the thoughts coming to my mind were not "me." This verse says there is a distinction between your thoughts and the intents of your heart. As I said, I loved God. The intent of my heart was to serve God and to please Him. I saw by revelation that I was a spirit. My spirit was the real me. The negative thoughts were not me. I could choose to reject those negative, condemning thoughts and cast them down.[41] Moreover, I could replace them by thinking and speaking the truth of God's Word.

The truth is: I am forgiven and cleansed by the blood of Jesus.[42] The truth is: I am a new creation in Christ![43] Hallelujah! Jesus said, *"You shall know the truth and the truth shall make you free."*[44] I learned that speaking God's Word is a powerful way to change my thinking, and bring freedom to my emotions.

Notice the first part of Hebrews 4:12: *"For the word of God is living and powerful, and sharper than any two-edged sword, piercing even to the division of soul and spirit."* The Word of God is alive! It has the power to penetrate and divide between soul and spirit. It is sharper than any two-edged sword. In Ephesians 6:17, God's Word is called *"the sword of the Spirit."* It cuts to the heart, to the spirit. It enables you to distinguish between what is of the soul and what is of the spirit. Only God's word has the power to do that.

---

[41] 2 Corinthians 10:4
[42] 1 John 1:9
[43] 2 Corinthians 5:17
[44] John 8:32

Recently my wife and I were eating at a fine dining restaurant. The waiter came to our table to serve the fish we had ordered. He took a sharp knife and removed the bones from the fish tableside. As you can imagine, fish bones are delicate so this was not an easy task, but he was able to accomplish it very quickly because he had a sharp knife and he was skilled. He had learned the technique and had practiced it. He was able to take the entire bone structure out in one piece. Of course, the whole point was presentation.

In Hebrews chapter five, we are encouraged to grow spiritually and become skillful in the word of righteousness, learning to handle God's Word properly and maturely. It says when we do we will have our senses exercised to discern both good and evil.[45] It is so important to spend time reading and meditating on God's Word, as well as listening to the Word being preached. As you become spiritually mature, growing in the knowledge of God's Word, it will become easier for you to use God's Word to distinguish between your soul and spirit. You will become skillful in discerning what is spiritual and what is mental, (what is scriptural and what is simply your own opinion or idea). This skill will help you make the right choices in life. Ultimately, you will be able to make a nice presentation of Jesus to the world!

Turn the Light On!

God's Words are spirit-Words because they are spoken by God who is a Spirit.[46] When God spoke the world into

---
[45] Hebrews 5:13-14
[46] John 4:24

THE REAL YOU

existence, He began by saying, *"Let there be light,"*[47] and there was light. When God's Word penetrates your spirit, the first thing that happens is the light comes on.

If you try to walk through a dark room in your house, you may stumble over a toy your child left in the middle of the floor. But if you turn the light on, you can see what obstacles may be in your way and avoid stubbing your toe. You can successfully navigate your way through the room. Psalm 119:105 says, *"Your word is a lamp to my feet and a light to my path."* Life becomes so much easier and more productive when the path in front of you is lit up by God's Word.

Proverbs 20:27 says, *"The spirit of man is the lamp of the Lord, searching all the inner depths of his heart."* This verse actually says our spirit is God's lamp. When Solomon wrote this proverb, a lamp was a candle. The King James Version says, *"The spirit of man is the candle of the Lord."* A few thousand years later, Thomas Edison invented the electric light bulb and now our lamps have light bulbs. The point is: God will enlighten you! He will "light your candle" or "turn on your light bulb." When that happens you can see what you are doing, what choices to make, and how to overcome life's difficulties.

David said in Psalm 18:28 (KJV), *"For thou wilt light my candle: the Lord my God will enlighten my darkness."* Most modern versions, including the New King James Version, say, *"For You will light my lamp."* In the next verse David

[47] Genesis 1:3

says what he can do after God lights his candle: *"For by You I can run against a troop, By my God I can leap over a wall."*[48] You can overcome every obstacle the enemy puts in your way once you have light from God's Word! You can do all things through Christ who strengthens you![49]

Paul's Prayer for Enlightenment

There is a Holy Spirit inspired prayer in Ephesians 1:17-20 that I pray often for others and for myself. It was a prayer prayed by the Apostle Paul, and it was recorded in Scripture so that we could pray it as well. It is God's Word, so it is alive and powerful:

> *That the God of our Lord Jesus Christ, the Father of glory, may give to you the spirit of wisdom and revelation in the knowledge of Him,* ***the eyes of your understanding being enlightened****; that you may know what is the hope of His calling, what are the riches of the glory of His inheritance in the saints, and what is the exceeding greatness of His power toward us who believe, according to the working of His mighty power which He worked in Christ when He raised Him from the dead and seated Him at His right hand in the heavenly places,*

Verse 18 says, *"the eyes of your understanding being enlightened."* The Amplified Bible says, *"having the eyes of your heart flooded with light."* There is a big difference

---
[48] Psalm 18:29
[49] Philippians 4:13

between a little night-light used in your bathroom in case someone has to get up in the middle of the night and a floodlight used to light up your entire back yard. The more light you have, the more you can see. Paul's prayer for the believers was for their hearts- their spirits- to be flooded with light. This is what we should desire and earnestly pray for.

What Does God's Word Say?

Remember, it is God's Word that brings light or spiritual understanding to our spirit. We can and should pray but without the knowledge of God's Word there will be very little light. If we are going to cast down imaginations and every high thing that exalts itself against the knowledge of God, as 2 Corinthians 10:4 tells us to, then we are going to have to have the knowledge of God in order to know what to cast down. We must have a revelation of God's Word in order to discern good and evil. When facing temptation or a difficult decision in life, we should ask the Holy Spirit, "What does God's Word say about this situation?" He will bring what you have read in the Bible to your remembrance.

I have known plenty of Christians who say they have prayed about God's will for them and they believe they have heard from God, but what they say God is leading them to do is contrary to the Bible. For example, a guy may become attracted to a girl who is not a Christian. The Bible says in 2 Corinthians 6:14, *"Do not be unequally yoked together with unbelievers."* He may want to marry the girl, but there's no use in praying about it. God's Word already has the answer. If she does not become a Christian, he needs to break off the relationship. *"What communion has light with darkness...or what part has a believer with an unbeliever?"* (2 Corinthians 6:14-15)

After my wife, Vicki, became a Christian as a teenager, she still continued to date unbelievers. Dating an unbeliever is dangerous. It's like a slippery creek bank. You may slide in if you hang around too long. Thankfully, Vicki became very hungry to know God's Word and spent hours reading the New Testament. She came across that passage in 2 Corinthians chapter 6 that says not to be unequally yoked together with unbelievers and she received a revelation of it. She said no one told her she shouldn't marry an unbeliever and she had not yet been taught it at church. She simply read her Bible and the Holy Spirit opened her eyes to the truth and the importance of marrying a believer. One guy actually proposed to her the day she left her hometown in Iowa to go to Bible School. He was not a Christian so she said no. I'm glad about that! She met me at Bible School.

Emotions run pretty deep and can sometimes be confused with God's leading, particularly when it comes to romantic relationships. If you're not careful, you will think the Holy Spirit is leading you to do something because you feel like its right and because you want to do it. This is why you need to not only pray, but study the Word of God and meditate on it until it draws a line of distinction between what is spiritual and what is emotional. When it comes to major decisions in your life, do not make impulsive choices that

THE REAL YOU

you may regret later. Instead, purposefully spend time in God's Word. Remember Psalm 119:105 says, *"Your Word is a lamp to my feet and a light to my path."*

Joints and Marrow

Now let's go back to Hebrews 4:12. In this verse, the soul and the spirit are illustrated as joints and marrow. The soul is like a joint. In Jesse Penn-Lewis' book, *"Soul and Spirit,"* she writes, *"In the threefold division of man's being, body, soul, and spirit, ...the due state in God's design is that the spirit which is the recipient of the Holy Spirit, uniting man to God, should be first, and should rule the soul,* **which stands intermediate between the body and the spirit."** The soul stands intermediate, like a joint, between the body and the spirit. This is why it is so important for you to possess your soul, bringing it into subjection to your spirit.

To illustrate this further, Jesus is called the only "mediator" between God and men.[50] He reconciles people to God, bringing them back into harmony with Himself. The soul is a "mediator" between the spirit and the body. When your soul is renewed to God's Word, it reconciles your body (your actions and your behavior) and brings your entire being back into harmony with your spirit, as God originally intended for it to be.

The marrow illustrates the spirit. The marrow in the human body is the flexible tissue in the interior of the bones where new blood cells are formed. Leviticus 17:11 says, *"The life*

[50] 1 Timothy 2:5

of the flesh is in the blood." The marrow is at the very center of our physical life. Likewise, the spirit is the very core of our spiritual life. Proverbs 4:23 says, *"Keep your heart with all diligence, For out of it spring the issues of life."*

The Laser of God's Word

With the advancement of medical science and technology, surgeons now are doing procedures with lasers. Laser light can be focused down to a tiny spot as small as a single wavelength. Webster's definition of laser is *"a device, containing a crystal gas, or other suitable substance, in which atoms, when stimulated by focused light waves, amplify and concentrate these waves, then emit them in a narrow, very intense beam."* Gas lasers are used to cut steel, as well as perform delicate eye surgery. Proverbs 20:27 in the New Living Translation says, *"The Lord's light penetrates the human spirit."* God's Word is brighter, more powerful, and more precise than a natural laser beam. Even though our spirit and our soul are closely related and intertwined, God's Word can penetrate and divide between them.

I like Jordon's paraphrase of Hebrews 4:12:

> *"God's word is alive with energy and sharper than any two-edged sword you ever saw. So sharp in fact that it can draw a line between the mental and the spiritual. In fact, it's like separating bones from marrow and discerns all our emotions and drives."*

The 20th Century translation, says, *"God's message is a*

THE REAL YOU

living, active power, piercing its way until it penetrates soul and spirit, not the joints only, but the very marrow."

When God's Word pierces to your spirit, something happens on the inside of you! Immediately, you become conscious of your spirit and of spiritual revelation. This revelation has the power to purify your soul and rid your mind of thoughts that would hinder you from fulfilling God's plan for your life.

Confession

Father, give to me the spirit of wisdom and revelation in the knowledge of Christ. Enlighten the eyes of my understanding that I may know what is the hope of Your calling and what are the riches of the glory of Your inheritance in the saints and what is the exceeding greatness of Your power toward me. In Jesus name, Amen.

Summary Questions

1. How is our soul like a joint?

2. How does God's Word compare to a sharp two-edged sword?

3. How could the prayer in Ephesians 1:17-20 help you distinguish between your soul and spirit?

4. How has God's Word been "a lamp unto your feet?" (Psalm 119:105)

CHAPTER 7

BECOMING SPIRIT CONSCIOUS

Keep your heart with all diligence, For out of it spring the issues of life. (Proverbs 4:23)

In order for your spirit to be the dominating force, ruling your soul and body, you must be consciously aware of your spirit; better said, you must become consciously aware that you are a spirit. I recommend two spiritual exercises that help me become spirit conscious: **1.) Praying in other tongues** and **2.) Meditating on God's Word.** If you will practice these and make them a part of your daily routine, you will be amazed at how much you will grow spiritually.

Praying in Tongues

The Apostle Paul said in 1 Corinthians 14:14, *"For if I pray in a tongue, my spirit prays, but my understanding is unfruitful."* Notice that Paul used the pronoun "I" when referring to his spirit. In other words, he used "I" and "my spirit" interchangeably. In essence, Paul was saying, "I

THE REAL YOU

am a spirit and my spirit prays in tongues." Tongues do not come from your mind; they come from your spirit. The Amplified Bible says, *"For if I pray in an [unknown] tongue, my spirit [by the Holy Spirit within me] prays, but my mind is unproductive [it bears no fruit and helps nobody]."* Praying in tongues is a spiritual exercise, not a mental exercise; therefore, praying in tongues will help you become spirit-conscious.

Remember Jesus' conversation with the woman at the well in Samaria?[51] He told her that He could give her living water that would be like a well inside of her. Later, in the seventh chapter of John's gospel,[52] Jesus stood up in the middle of a great Jewish feast and cried out with a loud voice, *"If anyone thirsts, let him come to Me and drink. He who believes in Me, as the Scripture has said, out of his heart will flow rivers of living water."*[53] The next verse says, *"But this He spoke concerning the Spirit, whom those believing in Him would receive."* (John 7:39) Jesus said these rivers would come out of the heart. We have already established that the heart is the spirit. The Amplified Bible says in verse 38, *"From his innermost being shall flow [continuously] springs and rivers of living water."*

I like how the Amplified version translates the spirit "innermost being." I also like how it says these rivers are to flow "continuously." When I went to Bible School in

---
[51] John 4:7-26
[52] John 7:37-38
[53] John 7:37-38

Tulsa, Oklahoma, I rented a room from a wonderful, elderly Christian lady. She had a Pentecostal church background, and many years before I met her she had been filled with the Holy Spirit and spoke in other tongues. However, she had the misunderstanding, as many other Christians have, that speaking in tongues was a one-time experience (unless the Holy Spirit comes upon you again in some special way and *makes you* speak in tongues). So even though she was a member of a Pentecostal church for decades, she had not taken advantage of the spiritual resource that was available on the inside of her. I was a young Bible school student, and she was in her eighties. I showed her from God's Word that she could speak in tongues anytime she chose. She received the truth and began praying in tongues on a regular basis.

The fact is every Christian can and should enjoy this experience continually. When you wake up in the morning, you can begin to speak in tongues. You don't need to just rely on coffee to perk you up; The Holy Spirit will perk you up!

Acts 2:4 says, *"And they were all filled with the Holy Spirit and began to speak with other tongues, as the Spirit gave them utterance."* "They" is the subject of the sentence, referring to the 120 believers who were filled with the Spirit. They did the speaking as the Holy Spirit gave them the words. Notice this verse also says, *"And they were ALL filled."* Every believer can be filled with the Holy Spirit and speak in tongues. In 1 Corinthians 14:15, the Apostle Paul said, *"I will pray with the spirit, and I will pray with the understanding also."* So, just like you can pray with

THE REAL YOU

your understanding at will, you can pray with your spirit at will.

If you are not familiar with speaking in other tongues, let me explain. The baptism in the Holy Spirit is available to everyone who is born again. I already quoted from John chapter seven where Jesus said those who believe in Him should receive the Holy Spirit.[54] Although you have a measure of the Holy Spirit when you receive Jesus as your Savior, there is a subsequent experience called "receiving the Holy Spirit," which is also called "being filled with the Holy Spirit" or "baptized in the Holy Spirit" (All three of these phrases are synonymous scriptural terms). When you are filled with the Holy Spirit you receive the supernatural ability to speak in other tongues (languages), unknown to you.[55] If you want to receive the gift of the Holy Spirit, ask God to fill you. Jesus said your Heavenly Father would give the Holy Spirit to them who ask Him.[56]

When you spend time praying in other tongues, take notice of where those tongues are coming from. If you were in a room full of people talking, and you recognized a particular person's voice that was speaking, but didn't see the person, you would listen and look to see where his or her words were coming from. Likewise, while you are praying in tongues, if you listen as well as "look" down on the inside of you, you will be able to locate your spirit, as it is your

---

[54] John 7:38
[55] See also Acts 10:44-46 and Acts 19:5-6
[56] Luke 11:13

spirit who is doing the speaking. If you were in a room full of people but everyone was quiet except for one person speaking, you would easily identify the source and be able to pay close attention to what was being said. This is what happens when you pray in tongues for a while. Your mind gets quiet, and there are no longer any distracting voices. You not only become spirit conscious, you begin to "see and hear" what the Holy Spirit is endeavoring to communicate.

Spiritual Strength Training

The Apostle Paul's earnest prayer for the believers in Ephesus was for them *"to be strengthened with might through His Spirit in the inner man."*[57] Remember the inner man is the real you. The book of Jude, verse 20, says, *"But you, beloved, building yourselves up on your most holy faith, praying in the Holy Spirit."* The word "yourself" in this verse refers to the real you - your spirit. When you pray in other tongues, you build yourself up spiritually. Physical exercise, particularly weight training, strengthens your muscles and builds up your outer man; in the same manner, praying in the Holy Spirit strengthens you spiritually and builds up your inner man.

The apostle Paul said in 1 Corinthians 14:4 *"He who speaks in a tongue edifies himself."* To edify means to build up. The New Living Translation says, "A person who speaks in tongues is strengthened." The Living Bible says, *"...a person speaking in tongues helps himself grow spiritually."* Paul made a habit of praying much in other tongues. He

[57] Ephesians 3:16

said in verse 18, *"I thank my God I speak with tongues more than you all."* We need to develop a habit of praying in tongues every day, never allowing "spiritual atrophy" to set in.

Another way to illustrate the building up of your spirit is to consider a battery that needs to be regularly charged. If you own a cellular phone, but forget to charge the battery, you may find yourself needing to answer (or finish) an important call, but your cell phone has insufficient power. The only way to remedy this problem is to get your phone to a power source to build it up again. We must keep our spirit built up in order to hear from God and communicate to others effectively on God's behalf. In fact, the next three verses after Jude 20 says, *"keep yourselves in the love of God, looking for the mercy of our Lord Jesus Christ unto eternal life. And on some have compassion, making a distinction; but others save with fear, pulling them out of the fire, hating even the garment defiled by the flesh."* By speaking in tongues, we not only keep ourselves built up, we keep ourselves in the love of God so that we may know how to effectively minister to others.

Spiritual Maintenance

Notice God's Word says *we* are to *build ourselves* up and *keep ourselves* in the love of God. Spiritual maintenance is our responsibility. God is not going to do this for us. We must choose to make a practice of praying in tongues and mediating on God's Word every day.

My wife's parents have a cabin on a lake in northern Minnesota. The outlet of the lake is on their property so a beautiful creek flows from the lake through their yard and back into the woods. My father-in-law is very diligent about maintaining his lakefront property and this creek. One summer while we were there visiting, some beavers tried to build a home in the culvert downstream from the lake. These beavers were persistent! Each night they labored cutting and gathering tree branches to dam up the culvert. But each and every morning my father-in-law put his rubber waders on, went into the creek and tore apart the dam they had built so the water would not back up and overflow onto his yard. He made sure the water level of the creek was maintained and the appropriate amount of water flowed over the river rocks, under the bridge, and through his property.

As Christians, we must be equally diligent in maintaining our spiritual landscape. Proverbs 4:23 says *"Keep your heart with all diligence, For out of it spring the issues of life."* Sometimes the devil works hard to build blockages in our minds and messes up our emotions in order to stop or hinder the flow of God's Spirit in and through our lives. The devil is called "the god of this world."[58] He gathers debris from various places - past experiences, secular music and television, ungodly relationships - and brings them to our minds. Like the beavers at my in-laws cabin, he is persistent! If you allow him to, he will set up house and build a stronghold in your soul. Every day we must

---
[58] 2 Corinthians 4:4

use God's Word to tear down what he tries to build up. Meditating on God's Word will tear down his work, and praying in the spirit will wash away the negative debris in your mind, allowing the rivers of life from your heart to flow freely through your soul and out into your actions.

Sometimes beavers will become "territorial," endeavoring to claim what they perceive to be their property. They will slap their smooth, wide tails against the water in defiance of anyone attempting to destroy "their home." In such a case, the property owner must demonstrate who is really in charge! Like the property owner, we must demonstrate who is really in charge. Remember James 4:7 says, *"Resist the devil and he will flee from you."*

Meditating on God's Word

The other spiritual exercise and means of becoming spirit conscious which I recommend is meditation on God's Word. To meditate, according to Strong's Exhaustive Concordance of the Bible, means "to ponder, imagine, speak, study, talk or utter." Like praying in tongues, your heart and your mouth are involved in this exercise. Meditation is not only thinking and pondering on God's Word, it is speaking it.

After the death of Moses, God commanded Joshua to lead the children of Israel into the Promised Land. There were many obstacles and adversities to overcome; therefore He repeatedly commanded him to be strong and courageous.[59]

---
[59] Joshua 1:6,7,9

In order to become and remain strong and courageous, God gave Joshua these important instructions:

"This Book of the Law shall not depart from your mouth, but you shall meditate in it day and night, that you may observe to do according to all that is written in it. For then you will make your way prosperous, and then you will have good success." (Joshua 1:8) The NAB version says, "Recite it by day and by night," and the Roth translation says, "talk to thyself therin day and night." God told Joshua that his success and prosperity were dependent upon his daily meditation in God's Word.

The Book of Psalms gives us similar instruction along with a similar promise of prosperity:

Blessed is the man
Who walks not in the counsel of the ungodly,
Nor stands in the path of sinners,
Nor sits in the seat of the scornful;
But his delight is in the law of the LORD,
And in His law he meditates day and night.
He shall be like a tree
Planted by the rivers of water,
That brings forth its fruit in its season,
Whose leaf also shall not wither;
And whatever he does shall prosper.
    (Psalm 1:1-3)

We understand the necessity of feeding and exercising our physical bodies in order to keep them strong and useful.

THE REAL YOU

Similarly, we must feed and exercise our spirits in order to be strong and useful spiritually. God's Word is spirit food. When Jesus was tempted by the devil to command stones to be made bread during his forty-day fast in the wilderness,[60] He overcame by quoting from Deuteronomy 8:3, *"Man shall not live by bread alone; but man lives by every word that proceeds from the mouth of the Lord."* Just like natural food has nutrients to strengthen and energize the body, God's Word has "spiritual nutrients" to strengthen and energize the spirit.

The Apostle John wrote in 1 John 2:14 *"you are strong, and the word of God abides in you, And you have overcome the wicked one."* When you meditate on God's Word your spirit is fed and nourished; you become strong spiritually and equipped to overcome temptation. In The Gospel of John, Jesus said, *"The words that I speak to you are spirit, and they are life."*[61] The Message Bible says, *"Every word I've spoken to you is a Spirit-word, and so it is life-making."* The Wade translation says, *"The words that I have spoken unto you are spiritual in their meaning and life giving in their effects."* As we meditate on God's Word, our spirit gets filled with God's life to the point of overflow. *Jesus said "I am come that they might have life, and that they might have it more abundantly."* John 10:10 Translators New Testament says *"that men may have life, and have it in overflowing measure."* Through meditation on God's Word we can experience our spirit overflowing with God's life.

[60] Matthew 4:1-4
[61] John 6:63

When your spirit is overflowing you become conscious of your spirit.

We must take the time to feed our spirits God's Word just like we take time to feed our bodies. Meditating in God's Word was one of the things that got Job through his excruciating trials; he said, *"I have treasured the words of His Mouth more than my necessary food."* (Job 23:12) Likewise, David's meditation on God's Word kept him from yielding to temptation during times of great trial; he said, *"Your word have I hidden in my heart, that I might not sin against You."* (Psalm 119:11)

A Proper Balance

You will be the most conscious of whichever one of your three-part being is being fed the most. For example, if you have to study for an important exam, you will become conscious of your mind. When you feed your body a good meal, you become conscious of your body. While mental and physical sustenance are important, we need a proper balance in our lives. Don't feed your mind and body at the expense of your spirit. Feeding and exercising your spirit will strengthen you and enable your spirit to dominate your soul and body, which is the key to living an effective and victorious Christian life. Decide right now to make time in your daily schedule to pray in tongues and meditate on God's Word. These two spiritual exercises will help you become conscious of *the real you*.

THE REAL YOU

Confession

Thank you Lord for the gift of the Holy Spirit, enabling me to pray in tongues and be spirit-conscious. Thank you for the power of Your Word and Your promise of good success as I meditate upon it. Thank you for helping me to incorporate these two practices into my daily routine so that I am able to stay strong in You and conscious of the real me.

Summary Questions

1. What are the two spiritual exercises that can help you become spirit conscious?

2. For someone who is baptized in the Holy Spirit, speaking in tongues should be

    a. A one-time experience or

    b. A continual experience?

3. How is praying in tongues similar to physical exercise?

4. According to Strong's Bible dictionary, what does meditation mean?

CHAPTER 8
RENEWING YOUR MIND

I beseech you therefore, brethren, by the mercies of God, that you present your bodies a living sacrifice, holy, acceptable to God, which is your reasonable service. And do not be conformed to this world, but be transformed by the renewing of your mind, that you may prove what is that good and acceptable and perfect will of God. (Romans 12:1-2)

In Romans chapter 12, verses one and two, we are admonished to do something with our body and with our mind. Paul is writing to Christians here and telling them how to experience the *"good and acceptable and perfect will of God."* He is saying that you must present your body to God and be transformed by renewing your mind. There is no other way to experience God's best for your life! No one, not even God, is going to do this for you. That's why Paul says, *"I beseech **you**."* Other translations say, *"I urge*

THE REAL YOU

you,"[62] or *"I plead with you."*[63]

In your spirit, you are a new creation.[64] In your spirit, you have been made the very righteousness of God in Christ.[65] You have everything it takes to live a victorious, overcoming, fulfilling life in Christ, but it is not automatic. You must get your mind renewed to these realities in order for them to be experienced in your life.

Metamorphosis

How does mind renewal take place? The Greek word translated "transformed" is metamorpho, which literally means to change into another form. We get the scientific term metamorphosis from this word; it is the process that a caterpillar goes through to become a butterfly. It's a transformation that takes place from the inside out. Conversely, the word *conformed* speaks of what happens to us from the outside if we allow it: *"Do not be **conformed** to this world, but be **transformed** by the renewing of your mind."* The Phillips translation says, *"Don't let the world around you squeeze you into its own mold, but let God remold your minds from within."*

This world has a way of putting pressure on you to

---

[62] NAS
[63] NLT
[64] 2 Corinthians 5:17
[65] 2 Corinthians 5:21

Renewing Your Mind

conform. There are so many influences in our everyday life: television, the Internet, social media, music, magazines, etc. Moreover, the most challenging influences come from our peers, our co-workers, family members, and friends who are not spiritual. This is why we are warned in scripture not to be close friends with unbelievers. That is not to say you shouldn't hang out with them in order to be a witness to them. However, if you are not influencing them, they are influencing you! You are being subtly squeezed into the mold of this world. The Bible says, *"Do not be deceived: 'Evil company corrupts good habits.'"*[66]

Psalm 1:1 (AMP) says, *"BLESSED (HAPPY, fortunate, prosperous, and enviable) is the man who walks and lives not in the counsel of the ungodly [following their advice, their plans and purposes], nor stands [submissive and inactive] in the path where sinners walk, nor sits down [to relax and rest] where the scornful [and the mockers] gather."*

God doesn't want you to just stay away from sinners; the key is to get your mind renewed to who you are in Christ so you can be a positive influence on others. People are watching your life. They want to know if Christianity is real and if it can make a difference in their life. While they are watching you, they're wondering: are they going to walk in integrity in this situation? Do they have genuine peace no matter what they're going through? Are they going to love me no matter how I treat them? People are looking

---

[66] 1Corinthians 15:33

for answers! Are you willing to be transformed so you can show them the way?

The Greek word, metamorpho, means, *"to change into another form" (meta, implying change, and morphe, "form:"), "the obligation being to undergo a complete change which, under the power of God, will find expression in character and conduct."*[67] This same Greek word is translated "transfigured" in Matthew 17:2 where Jesus was transfigured on the mountain before Peter, James, and John. What was on the inside of Him showed up on the outside, and *"His face shone like the sun, and his clothes became white as the light."*

Jesus looked like Adam looked before "The Fall," clothed with brilliant light. I'm not saying we can be transfigured in the exact same way Jesus was on the mount of transfiguration. Transformation is not going to happen instantly, or to the same degree, because Jesus was sinless; but we can undergo a process of transformation. We can be changed from the inside out, so that people can see Jesus on our countenance and in our lifestyle. Bruce's translation of Romans 12:2 says, *"What God is requiring of you is rather a complete transfiguration. This can be brought about if your minds receive a new directing power, enabling you to recognize what the will of God is."* The new directing power is your spirit, which has been born again!

Barkley's translation says, *"Your whole mental outlook must be radically altered."* I like that. Christianity is

[67] W. E. Vines Expository Dictionary of New Testament Words

radical! A caterpillar transformed into a butterfly is a major change! Perhaps you used to be a worm crawling on the ground, getting stomped on by life; now you're becoming a Monarch butterfly so you can fly high and free from the force of gravity and the confines of a cocoon! You are living the way God planned for you to live! You are experiencing the *"good, acceptable and perfect will of God."*

Do you know that most caterpillars never make it to the butterfly stage? There are too many outside influences that destroy their potential. Even if they make it to the cocoon stage, the elements of this world may corrode the cocoon and predators may eat the worm before it has a chance to fly. Many Christians don't reach their potential either.

Jordan's translation of Romans 12:2 says, *"Don't let the present age keep you in its cocoon."* You do not have to allow this world to keep you from becoming all God created you to be. It's time for you to break out of the cocoon! Break out of the mold! Be who you really are! You are a new creation in Christ! You are who God says you are; you have what God says you have; you can do what God says you can do!

Unveiling the New Model

Wuest's translation of Romans 12:2 paraphrases it this way, *"And stop assuming an outward expression that does not come from within you and is not representative of what you are in your inner being but is patterned after this age; but change your outward expression to one that comes from within and is representative of your inner being, by the renewing of your mind, resulting in your putting to the test what is the will of God, the good and well-pleasing and complete will, and having found that it meets specifications, place your approval upon it."*

Only as your mind is renewed can you accurately express who you are in your spirit, because your soul is the "joint" between your spirit and your body; it stands intermediate between the two. Remember that from chapter 6?

The sub-title of this book is "**Unveiling the Hidden Person of the Heart.**" Peter calls the spirit the "hidden person of the heart."[68] Your spirit is hidden to the natural eye, yet it can be unveiled in your character and conduct as your mind is renewed to God's Word. In 1 Peter verses 3 and 4, Peter says for wives to *"adorn"* themselves with *"the hidden person of the heart, with the incorruptible beauty of a gentle and quiet spirit, which is very precious in the sight of God."* Adorn means to display on the outside, just like one would wear beautiful jewelry. Peter says it's not the wearing of gold or the putting on of fine apparel that is going to win an unsaved husband to the Lord; it's the unveiling of a woman's gentle spirit.

One definition of unveil is to make public. Las Vegas hosts a number of car shows every year. Each year, at the Motor Trend International Auto Show, all the major manufacturers **unveil** their latest models. Thousands of people show up at The Convention Center to see what all the innovative and

[68] 1 Peter 3:4

creative minds in the auto industry have come up with. All the new models and redesigned vehicles are on display. It's actually pretty impressive. (We are so blessed in America! I remember going to Romania to preach in a Bible school just after Communism had fallen there. Nearly all the cars were the same. There was no creativity, no unique designs. If someone did get a new car imported from another country, everyone gathered around to see it.)

God has designed each of us uniquely with possibilities we have never even dreamed of. It's time to unveil His "new model" to the world. God has created you for display! He wants everyone around you to see how innovative your Creator is, and how uniquely He has designed you. 2 Corinthians 5:17 says, *"Therefore, if anyone is in Christ, he is a new creation."* The Amplified Bible says, *"a new creation all together."* There has never been a creation quite like you!

> *"For we are God's [own] handiwork (His workmanship), recreated in Christ Jesus, [born anew] that we may do those good works which God predestined (planned beforehand) for us [taking paths which He prepared ahead of time], that we should walk in them [living the good life which He prearranged and made ready for us to live]."* (Ephesians 2:10 AMP)

How can we live the good life God has prearranged and made ready for us to live? How can we unveil the hidden person of the heart to a world that is desperate to see something real? Can we really be changed from a caterpillar into a butterfly? *It's happening right now as you are reading this book!* It happens as you begin to see who you are in Christ. It happens as God's Word is revealed to your spirit.

Mind Renewal is a Process

Keep in mind that mind renewal is a process that takes time; it is not instant. However, be assured that every time you take the time to read or meditate on the Scriptures, or hear God's Word preached or taught, and you receive it with meekness, your mind is being renewed.

"Therefore lay aside all filthiness and overflow of wickedness, and receive with meekness the implanted word, which is able to save your souls." [69] James is writing to Christians, and he is talking to them about getting their souls saved. Your soul is not your spirit. James is <u>not</u> talking about being born again. The new birth is instant. The Greek word translated soul here is *psuche*. This word is also translated "mind" in other places in the scriptures. James is talking about the process of mind renewal. He calls it the saving of the soul.

According to James 1:21, mind renewal (or soul salvation) takes place when we receive God's Word with meekness (humility), allowing it to be implanted in our spirit. Mind renewal is more than memorizing Scriptures. I'm not discouraging you from memorizing Bible verses; that's a

---
[69] James 1:21

good practice. But I've met a lot of people who can quote Bible verses whose lives are really messed up! What I am saying is that mind renewal is not merely a mental exercise. Transformation takes place when the Word of God is implanted in your spirit and you receive a revelation of it. Then, when you act upon what is revealed, your mind is renewed in that particular area of your life. Your soul is then being saved. Thank God, no matter how messed up your life is, and no matter how badly damaged your soul may be, Jesus can save it, restore it, and renew it! David wrote in Psalm 23, verse 3, *"He restores my soul."*

Look in the Mirror!

The rest of the passage in James chapter one says,

> *But be doers of the word, and not hearers only, deceiving yourselves. For if anyone is a hearer of the word and not a doer, he is like a man observing his natural face in a mirror; for he observes himself, goes away, and immediately forgets what kind of man he was. But he who looks into the perfect law of liberty and continues in it, and is not a forgetful hearer but a doer of the work, this one will be blessed in what he does. (James 1:22-25)*

If you want to know what you look like, look in the mirror. What is true in the natural is also true in the spirit. God's Word is the mirror that reflects who you are on the inside -who you are in Christ. You're looking good in Christ! If you will spend time reading the New Testament, especially the

THE REAL YOU

Epistles (the letters written to the churches), you will find there are approximately 130 "in Christ" Scriptures. Look for the phrase, "in Christ" or "in Him" or "in Whom"—that's *the real you*. Also look for other little prepositional phrases such as "through Christ" and "by Christ." All these verses tell you who you are, what you have, and what you can do in and through Christ.

The New Testament is called "the perfect law of liberty." If you will continue in it, that is keep looking in the mirror of God's Word, you will be blessed in everything you do. On the other hand, a forgetful hearer of God's Word is like someone who only glances into the mirror and then walks away, forgetting what he or she looks like. If you forget who you are and what you really look like on the inside, you will begin to act like the person you used to be. Remember Wuest's translation of Romans 12:2: *"And stop assuming an outward expression that does not come from within you and is not representative of what you are in your inner being."*

Sanctification Through the Truth

The process of mind renewal is also called sanctification. Sanctify means to set apart for God's purpose, to make holy, to purify, or to consecrate. Paul prayed in 1 Thessalonians 5:23, *"Now may the God of peace Himself sanctify you completely; and may your whole spirit, soul, and body be preserved blameless at the coming of our Lord Jesus Christ."* This is God's will for our lives! He wants us to be sanctified completely -spirit, soul and body.

In the Gospel of John, just before he was betrayed and turned over to the chief priests and Pharisees, Jesus prayed for His disciples and for all of us who would believe in Him through their word. He said to the Father, *"Sanctify them by your truth. Your Word is truth."* (John 17:17)

When you heard the truth of the gospel and received Jesus Christ as your personal Lord and Savior, your spirit was instantly sanctified. You were made holy in Christ when you were born again. Ephesians 4:24 says, *"the new man... was created according to God, in true righteousness and holiness."* Your soul, however, is in the *process* of sanctification. As you receive and act upon the truth of God's Word, your soul is sanctified. Finally, as your mind is renewed, your body and your behavior become sanctified. Paul's prayer was for this process to continue right up until the return of Jesus Christ. When Christ returns, we will receive a new body like Jesus' glorified body and our salvation will be complete!

Confession

God I present myself to You allowing You to sanctify me completely - spirit, soul and body. I choose not to be conformed to the world, but to be transformed by the renewing of my mind. My whole mental outlook is being radically altered. Thank You Lord that I am able to see what is good and pleasing in Your sight and live accordingly. As my mind is renewed I am able to accurately express

THE REAL YOU

who I am in my spirit and unveil this new person to the world. Thank You for helping me to live the good life You have designed for me and transforming me into something beautiful and worthy of You.

Summary Questions

1. Describe how mind renewal is more than memorizing scripture.

2. Are there people and/or influences in your life that have kept you "conformed to this world?" What steps can you take to change this?

3. What is sanctification? Describe how and when your spirit, soul and body are sanctified.

4. What positive results can you expect to see in your life as you "unveil the hidden person of the heart?"

CHAPTER 9

FLESH VS. SPIRIT

There is therefore now no condemnation to those who are in Christ Jesus, who do not walk according to the flesh, but according to the Spirit. For the law of the Spirit of life in Christ Jesus has made me free from the law of sin and death. (Romans 8:1-2)

When Adam sinned, "the law of sin and death" came into effect for the entire human race. God had commanded Adam and given him a warning, *"Of every tree of the garden you may freely eat; but of the tree of the knowledge of good and evil you shall not eat,* **for in the day** *that you eat of it* **you shall surely die."** (Genesis 2:16-17) Adam did not die physically the day he ate of the fruit. As a matter of fact, he lived to be 930 years old. So what happened? In what way did he die?

The day Adam disobeyed God's command, he died spiritually; his spirit was separated from God. Death began exerting control over his soul and body. Fear, confusion, shame, and condemnation replaced the sweet peace and fellowship he had enjoyed with God every day. Adam's body was designed to live forever, but *in the day* he ate that fruit, it became mortal- subject to the law of sin and death, and began to decay. Eventually he died physically.

Because Adam was the head of the human race, every person born into the earth was born with a mortal body. In addition, there was an element of sin passed down through the flesh. *"Through one man sin entered the world, and death through sin, and thus death spread to all men, because all sinned."* (Romans 5:12)

The good news is, ***"the law of the Spirit of life in Christ Jesus has made us free from the law of sin and death."***[70] When we are born again, the Spirit of life comes into our spirit and sets us free from the law of sin and death! We no longer have to be dominated by sin. A new law has come into effect in our spirit. The Phillips translation says, *"For the new spiritual principle of life lifts me out of the old vicious circle of sin and death."* Romans 6:14 says, *"For sin shall not have dominion over you, for you are not under the law, but under grace."*

Paul describes the vicious circle of sin and death in Romans chapter seven. As a Jew under the law, he sincerely delighted in the law of God, but he explained that the law of sin in his members held him captive, keeping him from doing everything the law required. He said, *"in my flesh dwells no*

---

[70] Romans 8:2

good thing."[71] Chapter seven ends with this exclamation: *"O wretched man that I am! Who will deliver me from this body of death?"* He immediately answers, *"I thank God through Jesus Christ our Lord!"*[72]

No Condemnation!

The key to living free from condemnation and from the law of sin and death is walking according to the Spirit.[73] Jesus Christ has made a way, through His death and resurrection, for us to live the way God intended for us to live: with our spirit as the dominating force and our body merely acting as the instrument of the spirit, through the soul. The law of the Spirit of life in Christ Jesus can now become the governing force of our actions.

God does not want any believer to live under condemnation. The Holy Spirit will convict us if we have sinned in order to bring us to repentance, but he does not condemn us. There is a difference. Condemnation brings discouragement and hopelessness. The Bible says the goodness of God leads us to repentance.[74] Repentance is an action of the will, which is part of our soul. It is a decision to turn from sin and turn to God in response to His grace. It is a change of direction, which results in blessing.

The devil tries to use condemnation and shame to hinder us from being everything God wants us to be. He tries to

[71] Romans 7:18
[72] Romans 7:14-25
[73] Romans 8:1
[74] Romans 2:4

paralyze our effectiveness through guilt and shame. He is a liar and a defeated foe! Jesus bore our sin and shame. We can receive forgiveness and cleansing for sin[75] and deliverance from shame. We can walk free from condemnation by walking according to the Spirit.

"For God did not send His Son into the world to condemn the world, but that the world through Him might be saved." (John 3:17)

A Better Covenant

For what the law could not do in that it was weak through the flesh, God did by sending His own Son in the likeness of sinful flesh, on account of sin: He condemned sin in the flesh, that the righteous requirement of the law might be fulfilled in us who do not walk according to the flesh but according to the Spirit. (Romans 8:3-4)

The Old Testament law curbed man's sinful behavior, but it could not do what only Jesus Christ could do: take away our sin and give us the Spirit of life in its place! *"For God has done what the Law could not do, [its power] being weakened by the flesh [the entire nature of man without the Holy Spirit]. Sending His own Son in the guise of sinful flesh and as an offering for sin, [God] condemned sin in the flesh [subdued, overcame, deprived it of its power over all who accept that sacrifice], [Leviticus 7:37.]."* (Romans 3:20 AMP)

[75] 1 John 1:9

The redemptive work of Christ subdued, overcame, and deprived sin of its power over the Christian!

Your Sins Are Gone!

Under the law of the Old Testament, the blood of animal sacrifices covered man's sin for a season, but could never take away sin. Each year the High Priest would have to enter the Holy of Holies again with the blood of bulls and goats (Hebrews 10:3-4). In contrast, Hebrews 9:12-14 says,

> *Not with the blood of goats and calves, but with His own blood He entered the Most Holy Place once for all, having obtained eternal redemption. For if the blood of bulls and goats and the ashes of a heifer, sprinkling the unclean, sanctifies for the purifying of the flesh, how much more shall the blood of Christ, who through the eternal Spirit offered Himself without spot to God, cleanse your conscience from dead works to serve the living God?*

Hebrews 10:14 says, *"For by one offering He has perfected forever those who are being sanctified."*

When John the Baptist saw Jesus coming to The Jordan River to be baptized he said, *"Behold! The Lamb of God who takes away the sin of the world!"* (John 1:29) Jesus didn't just cover your sins: He took them away! All your sins are gone!

We have a new and better covenant, established on better

promises.[76] Jeremiah prophesied concerning this New Covenant: *"But this is the covenant that I will make with the house of Israel after those days, says the Lord: I will put My law in their minds, and write it on their hearts;"* (Jeremiah 31:33) Ezekiel also prophesied regarding this New Covenant: *"I will give you a new heart and put a new spirit within you; I will take the heart of stone out of your flesh and give you a heart of flesh. I will put My Spirit within you and cause you to walk in My statutes, and you will keep My judgments and do them."* (Ezekiel 36:26-27)

These prophecies have been fulfilled in Christ. What the law could not do because of the weakness of man's flesh, Jesus <u>did</u> do through His death and resurrection. We have a new heart, a new spirit. God has inscribed His law on our inner man. We no longer have to struggle, depending on our own strength or will power to meet up to God's standard of righteousness. In fact, no one has ever met up to it outside of Christ. "All have missed the mark and fallen short of God's glorious intention for them." (Romans 3:23 Translators N.T.)

The law of the Spirit of life in Christ Jesus provided the solution. In Christ, we have been made the righteousness of God.[77] Look again at verse four of Romans 8: *"**that the righteous requirement of the law might be fulfilled in us who do not walk according to the flesh but according to the Spirit.**"*

---

[76] Hebrews 8:6
[77] 2 Corinthians 5:21

Circumcision of the Heart

Both the Old and New Covenants were ratified through the shedding of blood. "For without the shedding of blood there is no forgiveness."[78] The Covenant God made with Abraham was sealed with circumcision. The Covenant God made with Jesus Christ was ratified through His shed blood, and for all who would accept His sacrifice; this New Covenant is sealed with a spiritual circumcision - <u>the new birth</u>. The new birth is a circumcision of the heart.

Consider these New Testament scriptures:

*"For he is not a Jew who is one outwardly, nor is circumcision that which is outward in the flesh; but he is a Jew who is one inwardly; and circumcision is that **of the heart, in the Spirit.**"* (Romans 2:28)

*"For we are the circumcision, who worship God **in the Spirit**, rejoice in Christ Jesus, and have no confidence in the flesh."* (Philippians 3:3)

*"For in Christ Jesus neither circumcision nor uncircumcision avails anything, but **a new creation.**"* (Galatians 6:15)

What is the Flesh?

It is unfortunate that some Bible teachers and even some Bible translators refer to "the flesh" as your "sinful nature" or "carnal nature" because that implies that you have two

---

[78] Hebrews 9:22

natures. That terminology is confusing. I mean no disrespect to certain translators of the Bible, but I don't agree with their interpretation. Spiritually, you have only one nature.

You are a spirit, you have a soul, and you live in a body. Your spirit is the real you and if you are born again, your spirit is a new creation in Christ. You do not have two natures at war with each other inside your body. The "war" is between your spirit and what the Bible calls "the flesh." Walking "according to the flesh" is allowing your body (influenced by the world through your five physical senses) and your un-renewed mind to dominate you rather than being controlled by your born again spirit. You are free from the law of sin and death in your spirit, but the key to *living free* from sin and its consequences is walking according to the Spirit, and not according to the flesh.

What is "the flesh?" "The flesh" in scripture refers to our propensity toward evil because of the element of sin that resides in our mortal bodies. The works of the flesh are listed in Galatians 5:19-21: *"Now the works of the flesh are evident, which are: adultery, fornication, uncleanness, lewdness, idolatry, sorcery, hatred, contentions, jealousies, outbursts of wrath, selfish ambitions, dissensions, heresies, envy, murders, drunkenness, revelries, and the like..."*

Which One Will Win?

Romans chapter 8, verse 5 says: *"For those who live according to the flesh set their minds on the things of the flesh, but those who live according to the Spirit, the things of the Spirit."*

If you set your mind on the things of the flesh, you will live according to the flesh; the flesh wins. If you set your mind on the things of the Spirit, you will live according to the Spirit; the spirit wins. It's that simple! Colossians 3:1-2 says, *"If then you were raised with Christ, seek those things which are above, where Christ is, sitting at the right hand of God.* **Set your mind on things above***, not on things on the earth. For you died, and your life is hidden with Christ in God."*

Remember, your soul is the "joint." It stands intermediate between your spirit and your body. Your soul either sides in with "the flesh," **or** it comes into harmony with *the real you* - your spirit. Your soul is the determining factor in the equation: two against one = majority rules.

Carnal Mind vs. Spiritual Mind

Romans 8:6 says, **"For to be carnally minded is death, but to be spiritually minded is life and peace."** The NIV says, *"The mind governed by the flesh is death, but the mind governed by the Spirit is life and peace."* The question is, which one will govern your mind- the flesh or the Spirit? The answer is whichever one you set your mind on or give your attention to will govern. A carnal (fleshly) mind will produce death in your life in some form and to some degree. A spiritual mind will produce life and peace. If you want to experience life and peace you must become spiritually

THE REAL YOU

minded, by setting your mind on the things of the Spirit.

In other words, you must intentionally develop habits that renew your mind to God's Word, like reading your Bible and attending church to hear God's Word preached and taught. In addition, worshipping God, fellowshipping with other Christians and sharing your faith will help you to set your mind on things above. I especially encourage you to make a practice of meditating on who you are in Christ. *Life and peace await you!*

As you continue reading in the eighth chapter of Romans you'll find that "the carnal mind is enmity against God. It is not subject to God's law nor can it be."[79] This is why we must be committed to getting our minds renewed. Verse 8 says "those who are in the flesh cannot please God. But you are not in the flesh, if indeed the Spirit of God dwells in you."[80]

Romans 8:10 says, **"And if Christ is in you, the body is dead because of sin, but the Spirit is life because of righteousness."** Although your body is mortal and will eventually die because of sin, your spirit is alive with God's life because of the righteousness Jesus Christ produced through his death and resurrection. Ephesians 2:1 says, *"And you He made alive,* who were dead in trespasses and sins.*"*

Romans 8:11 says, **"But if the Spirit of Him who raised Jesus from the dead dwells in you, He who raised Christ**

---

[79] Romans 8:7
[80] Romans 8:9

from the dead will also give life to your mortal bodies through His Spirit who dwells in you."

Even though your body is mortal and will not be fully redeemed until Christ's return, it can be affected by God's resurrection life that is in your spirit. The Holy Spirit will give life to your mortal body, keeping it free to be the instrument of your spirit. Romans 6:12-13 says, *"Therefore do not let sin reign in your mortal body, that you should obey it in its lusts. And do not present your members as instruments of unrighteousness to sin, but present yourselves to God as being alive from the dead, and your members as instruments of righteousness to God."*

When the Apostle Paul was undergoing intense persecution for the sake of the gospel, he said, *"But we have this treasure in earthen vessels, that the excellence of the power may be of God and not of us. We are hard-pressed on every side, yet not crushed; we are perplexed, but not in despair; persecuted, but not forsaken; struck down, but not destroyed— always carrying about in the body the dying of the Lord Jesus,* ***that the life of Jesus also may be manifested in our body.****"* (2 Corinthians 4:7-10)

This great treasure we have in our "earthen vessels" is the life of Jesus, which can be manifested in and through our bodies no matter what kind of trial we may be enduring. Our greater goal as Christians is not to simply overcome the trial for our own sake, but to manifest Jesus to the world at all times. The Amplified Bible says, *"so that the*

THE REAL YOU

[resurrection] life of Jesus also may be shown forth by and in our bodies."

A spiritual mind is one that is being constantly renewed to God's Word. See yourself as God sees you by continually looking into the mirror of God's Word. See yourself as you really are in Christ: a new creation,[81] the righteousness of God,[82] more than a conqueror.[83] As you meditate on these truths (speak these truths to yourself), you will have a spiritual mind, you will keep your body under subjection to your spirit, and you will manifest the life of Jesus to the world.

Kill the Deeds of the Body and Live

Finally, verses 12-13 of Romans 8 say, *"Therefore, brethren, we are debtors—not to the flesh, to live according to the flesh. For if you live according to the flesh you will die; but if by the Spirit you put to death the deeds of the body, you will live."*

You don't owe your flesh anything! We are not debtors to the flesh. If your flesh wants to be mean and retaliate against someone who has hurt you, you are under no obligation to respond. You can remind yourself that the love of God has been shed abroad in your heart by the Holy Spirit.[84] If your flesh wants to mope all day, and you're feeling discouraged and sorry for yourself, you can say, "No, thank you! I believe

---
[81] 2 Corinthians 5:17
[82] 2 Corinthians 5:21
[83] Romans 8:37
[84] Romans 5:5

Flesh vs. Spirit

I'll just go ahead and get happy.[85] The joy of the Lord is my strength!"[86] If your flesh wants to indulge in pornography, alcohol, or fornication (sex outside of marriage), you can boldly say, "I am a new creation; sin cannot dominate me."[87]

By reminding yourself of who you are, you "put to death" the deeds of the body. You kill your old ways of thinking and your old ways of acting according to the flesh. Every time you make a choice to speak God's Word and act on God's Word you "live!" You yield yourself to the help of the Holy Spirit, and you release the life of God from your spirit. You purify your soul and renew your mind. You will experience life and peace.[88]

Confession

I am in Christ Jesus and there is therefore now no condemnation. The law of the spirit of life in Christ Jesus has made me free from the law of sin and death. Sin has been deprived of its power over me. I don't owe my flesh anything. I am a new creation. I walk in the spirit and put to death the deeds of the body.

Summary Questions

1. Describe the "vicious" circle of sin and death that Paul wrote about in Romans chapter 7.

---

[85] Philippians 4:4
[86] Nehemiah 8:10
[87] 2 Corinthians 5:17
[88] Romans 8:6

THE REAL YOU

2. What is the difference between conviction and condemnation?

3. Repentance is an action of the _____, which is part of our soul.

4. What is "circumcision of the heart?" Has your heart been circumcised?

5. Why is it a bad idea to refer to "the flesh" as your "sinful nature?"

6. I am a _____, I have a _____, and I live in a _____.

CHAPTER 10

SERVING GOD WITH YOUR SPIRIT

"For God is my witness, whom I serve with my spirit in the gospel of His Son, that without ceasing I make mention of you always in my prayers." (Romans 1:9)

Paul said, *"God is my witness, whom I **serve with my spirit**."* He was not saying that his soul and body were left out in his service to God; he was simply saying that his spirit was at the center of it all. His spirit was the directing force of his life and service. When we consider the variety of activities involved in serving God, we understand that Paul was actually saying, "I worship God *with my spirit*, I fellowship with God *with my spirit*, I pray *with my spirit*, I receive revelation and guidance *with my spirit*, and I obey God *with my spirit*.

T. Austin Sparks, in his book, "What is Man?" said, *"Having seen that the basis of all fellowship and co-operation with*

THE REAL YOU

God is spiritual, in and through the born-again spirit, we must realize that this at once defines the real nature of our service."[89]

Romans 8:14-17 says, *"For as many as are led by the Spirit of God, these are sons of God. For you did not receive the spirit of bondage again to fear, but you received the Spirit of adoption by whom we cry out, "Abba, Father." The Spirit Himself bears witness <u>with our spirit</u> that we are children of God."*

You know in your spirit that you are a child of God because the Holy Spirit "bears witness" with your spirit. You have God's life and nature in your spirit. Peter said we have become "partakers of the divine nature."[90] God is your very own Father.

The Psalmist declared:

> *"When I consider Your heavens, the work of Your fingers, The moon and the stars, which You have ordained; What is man that You take thought of him, And the son of man that You care for him? Yet You have made him a little lower than God, And You crown him with glory and majesty!" (Psalms 8:4-5)*

In chapter one, "You Are God's Design," we established that God created Adam and Eve in His image to have dominion. When you were born again, God re-created you in His image to have dominion. Through the new birth,

---
[89] p. 124
[90] 2 Peter 1:4

God's original intent of the order of your spirit, soul and body became restored. Sin shall no longer have dominion over you.[91] The real you is to reign as a king in life (Zoé) through Jesus Christ.[92]

As you serve God with your spirit, you will live life to the fullest. This doesn't mean that life will be without challenge. As long as you are in this world, Jesus said you will have tribulation. But he also said, "Be of good cheer, I have overcome the world." (John 16:33) The reason we can get happy about the fact that Jesus overcame the world is because He overcame it for us and we are now in Him. We are His workmanship and we really can live the good life He has made ready for us to live.

> *For we are God's [own] handiwork (His workmanship), recreated in Christ Jesus, [born anew] that we may do those good works which God predestined (planned beforehand) for us [taking paths which He prepared ahead of time], that we should walk in them [living the good life which He prearranged and made ready for us to live]. (Ephesians 2:10 AMP)*

Living Life Abundantly

"For he who sows to his flesh will of the flesh reap corruption, but he who sows to the Spirit will of the Spirit reap everlasting life." (Galatians 6:8)

---

[91] Romans 6:14
[92] Romans 5:17

THE REAL YOU

Sowing to the spirit will cause you to reap a harvest of everlasting life. What does it mean to reap everlasting life? First we must define everlasting life.

The word *life* is a BIG word in the New Testament. One of the Greek words translated life is Zoé. It means life as God has it. Remember, mankind was spiritually dead as a result of "The Fall," so Jesus came to give us life (Zoé).[93] 1 John 5:11-12 says, *"And this is the testimony: that God has given us **eternal life**, and this **life** is in His Son.* ***He who has the Son has life; he who does not have the Son of God does not have life.****"*

Here's what W. E. Vines Dictionary says about the Greek word Zoé translated life: *"Zoé is used in the New Testament of life as a principle, life in the absolute sense, life as God has it, that which the Father has in Himself, and which He gave to the Incarnate Son to have in Himself, John 5:26, and which the Son manifested in the world, 1 John 1:2. From this life man has become alienated in consequence of the Fall, Ephesians 4:18, and of this life men become partakers through faith in the Lord Jesus Christ."*

In reference to eternal life, a note from the Translators New Testament says, *"The word eternal draws attention to the quality of that life, not to its duration in a temporal sense."* William Barclay's Commentary explains, *"Eternal life is not simply life that goes on forever. It is true that the New Testament never forgets that God has promised men resurrection from the dead, but the essential of eternal life*

[93] John 3:16

is not duration, it is quality."

Zoé is the best quality of life there is; it is absolute life, life as God has it! Absolute means pure -free from mixture. In physics, absolute cold or absolute zero is the lowest possible temperature, at which point the atoms of a substance transmit no thermal energy. They are completely at rest; there is absolutely no heat. 1 John 1:5 says, *"God is light and in Him is no darkness at all."* God is also life[94] and in Him is no death at all. This is the quality of life God has imparted to your spirit. It is hell busting, devil-defeating life! It is God's life!

Life in Overflowing Measure

Life (Zoé) is measurable. You can have more or less of it. Jesus said, *"I have come that they may have **life**, and that they may have it **more abundantly**."* (John 10:10) William's translation says, *"I have come for people to have life and have it **till it overflows**."* Translator's N.T. says, *"that men may have life, and have it **in overflowing measure**."*

Galatians 6:7-8 says that if we sow to the spirit, we will reap everlasting life. ***Your spirit is the seed ground for God's Word.*** If you will sow God's Word into your spirit, you will reap a harvest of life (Zoé). You determine how much of the fruits of the Spirit you will reap; you determine how much Zoé life you live. You can actually experience *"life more abundantly," "life til it overflows,"* or *"life in overflowing measure."* Jesus said, *"It is the Spirit who gives life; the*

[94] 1 John 5:20

THE REAL YOU

flesh profits nothing. The words that I speak to you are spirit, and they are life." (John 6:63) The Message Bible says, *"Every word I've spoken to you is a Spirit-word, and so it is life-making."*

What Type of Soil Are You?

In the Parable of the Sower,[95] Jesus illustrated spiritual growth with four types of soil. He explained that the seed is the Word of God. He said the birds of the air came and devoured the seed that was sown on *hard ground*. (The birds represent Satan, the devourer.) Next, he said the sun (tribulation and persecution) scorched the tender plants sown on *stony ground* because they had no roots. Thirdly, thistles choked the plants that grew on *thorny ground* (The thorns are the cares of this world, the deceitfulness of riches, and the desire for other things). None of these three types of soil bore any fruit. According to Jesus, *only one* type of soil produced fruit. The *good ground*, He said, are the people who "hear the Word, accept it, and bear fruit: some thirtyfold, some sixty, and some a hundred."[96]

According to Jesus' parable, only a small percentage of people who are privileged to hear God's Word actually become fruitful Christians. That's because we have our part to play. It's not all up to God. It's up to us to hear the Word, and act on it, so that the life of God (Zoé) that is contained in the seed of His Word will take root in our hearts and

---

[95] Mark 4
[96] Mark 4:20

renew our minds. Only then will our lives produce fruit that is attractive to others, potentially leading them to Christ, causing multiplication of the seed sown in us.

The Fruit of the Spirit

Galatians 5:16 says, *"Walk in the Spirit, and you shall not fulfill the lusts of the flesh."* Notice this verse does not say, "Don't fulfill the lusts of the flesh and you will be walking in the Spirit." The emphasis of the instruction is to walk in the Spirit. Many Christians focus on what not to do; instead, we should focus on walking in the spirit and then we will not fulfill the lusts of the flesh. The fruit of the Spirit, according to Galatians 5:22 and 23 is *"love, joy, peace, longsuffering, kindness, goodness, faithfulness, gentleness, and self-control."*

God is Love

"Abide in Me, and I in you. As the branch cannot bear fruit of itself, unless it abides in the vine, neither can you, unless you abide in Me. I am the vine, you are the branches. He who abides in Me, and I in him, bears much fruit; for without Me you can do nothing." (John 15:4-5)

Jesus made it clear that we cannot bear fruit of ourselves. Fruitfulness as Christians depends upon our fellowship and communion with Him. In John chapter 15, verse nine, Jesus said, *"As the Father loved me, I also have loved you; abide in My love."* Really all of the fruit of the spirit is love. So the fruit we need to cultivate in our lives is love. If you compare the fruits listed in Galatians 5 with the description of love in 1 Corinthians 13, the "love chapter," you will find them to be almost identical. To walk in the Spirit is to walk in love because *"God is love."*[97]

The more of God's Word you sow into your spirit by meditating on it, hearing it and acting on it, the more life you will experience. I challenge you to meditate on 1 Corinthians 13:4-8 every day for a month and see what it will do for your love life!

Remember what Psalm one, verses 2 & 3 say? The person who meditates day and night in God's Word will be like a tree planted by rivers of water. Water is illustrative of life. It says this person will bring forth fruit, and whatever he does shall prosper.[98] A tree doesn't struggle to bear fruit when it has a sufficient water supply. If you are drinking from the water of the Word you will not struggle to bear fruit. F.F. Bosworth, in his book, "Christ the Healer," said this about Zoé: *"The life of God received in sufficient measure lives itself."*

Open Up the Valve!

The primary water supply for Las Vegas comes from Lake Mead, which is one of the largest man-made lakes in the world, formed by the Hoover Dam and fed by the Colorado River. It's a pretty big water source. The water is piped to homes all over the Las Vegas Valley. If the valve to the main water source is shut off, you can live in a home connected

---
[97] 1 John 4:8
[98] Psalms 1:2 & 3

Serving God with Your Spirit

to the source and never enjoy the water. A valve is a device that permits the flow of water in one direction only. The pressure and the supply are there all the time; you just need to open the valve.

Your spirit is connected to Jesus. *"He who is joined to the Lord is one spirit with Him."*[99] He is the source of living water! Jesus said, *"He who believes in Me, as the Scripture has said, out of his heart will flow rivers of living water."*[100] Your soul is the valve. The water pressure and all the supply you need is on tap. All you need to do is open the valve by speaking God's Word and praying in the Holy Spirit. Another way to get the water flowing is by sharing Jesus with others. *"He who waters will also be watered himself."* (Proverbs 11:25)

The water level at Lake Mead has dropped significantly over the years, but the first year after we moved to Las Vegas, in 1983, they opened up the spillways at Hoover Dam to prevent flooding and over-topping. It was the first time they had opened them since 1941 (when they opened them for testing). We drove out to see the water gush through the tunnels. It really was a sight to behold. Each gate weighs 5 million pounds. I thought about Jesus saying He came to give us life more abundantly, life in overflowing measure. Do you think maybe the church could experience more power than we have experienced? I think so! Do you think *you* could experience more of the life of Jesus?

---

[99] 1 Corinthians 6:17
[100] John 7:37

THE REAL YOU

I trust this book has encouraged you to see yourself the way God sees you. Now unveil the hidden person of your heart to your world; live your life as ***The Real You***.

Confession

I am God's own handiwork, recreated in Christ Jesus that I may do those good works, which God pre-destined for me. I choose to serve God with my spirit and live the good life He has made ready for me to live. Thank You Lord, for Zoé- absolutely pure, eternal life that You have imparted to my spirit. I will sow Your Word into my spirit and reap an abundant harvest of life and love.

Summary Questions

1. What does it mean to serve God with your spirit?

2. According to John 16:30, we are not promised a life without tribulation; but Jesus said to be of good cheer. Why? How did Jesus provide hope to Christians living in a fallen world?

3. What kind of life is *Zoé* life?

4. In the Parable of the Sower, what type of soil produced fruit? What type of soil are you?

5. Which fruit of the spirit would you like to see more production of in your life? What must you sow into your spirit in order to produce the fruit you desire?

SCRIPTURES

Here are some of the "Real You" scriptures I shared in this book. I encourage you to use them by meditating on them and confessing them out loud. Philemon 1:6 says, "That the sharing of your faith may become effective by the acknowledgement of every good thing which is in you in Christ Jesus." Confessing these scriptures will help you overcome your fears, insecurities, disappointments or any obstacles life may have thrown your way and ultimately help you to discover The Real You.

Genesis 1:26-28
Then God said, "Let Us make man in Our image, according to Our likeness; let them have dominion over the fish of the sea, over the birds of the air, and over the cattle, over all the earth and over every creeping thing that creeps on the earth." So God created man in His own image; in the image of God He created him; male and female He created them. Then God blessed them, and God said to them, "Be fruitful and multiply; fill the earth and subdue it; have dominion over the fish of the sea, over the birds of the air, and over every living thing that moves on the earth."

Genesis 2:7
And the LORD God formed man of the dust of the ground, and breathed into his nostrils the breath of life;

and man became a living being.

Joshua 1:8
This Book of the Law shall not depart from your mouth, but you shall meditate in it day and night, that you may observe to do according to all that is written in it. For then you will make your way prosperous, and then you will have good success.

1 Samuel 16:7
But the LORD said to Samuel, "Do not look at his appearance or at his physical stature, because I have refused him. For the LORD does not see as man sees; for man looks at the outward appearance, but the LORD looks at the heart.

Job 32:8
But there is a spirit in man, And the breath of the Almighty gives him understanding.

Psalms 1:1-3
Blessed is the man Who walks not in the counsel of the ungodly, Nor stands in the path of sinners, Nor sits in the seat of the scornful; But his delight is in the law of the LORD, And in His law he meditates day and night. He shall be like a tree Planted by the rivers of water, That

brings forth its fruit in its season, Whose leaf also shall not wither; And whatever he does shall prosper.

Psalms 8:3-5
When I consider Your heavens, the work of Your fingers, The moon and the stars, which You have ordained, What is man that You are mindful of him, And the son of man that You visit him? For You have made him a little lower than the angels, And You have crowned him with glory and honor.

Proverbs 4:23
Keep your heart with all diligence, For out of it spring the issues of life.

Proverbs 20:27
The spirit of a man is the lamp of the LORD, Searching all the inner depths of his heart.

Luke 21:19
By your patience possess your souls.

John 3:3-7
Jesus answered and said to him, "Most assuredly, I say

THE REAL YOU

to you, unless one is born again, he cannot see the kingdom of God." Nicodemus said to Him, "How can a man be born when he is old? Can he enter a second time into his mother's womb and be born?" Jesus answered, "Most assuredly, I say to you, unless one is born of water and the Spirit, he cannot enter the kingdom of God. That which is born of the flesh is flesh, and that which is born of the Spirit is spirit. Do not marvel that I said to you, "You must be born again."

John 4:24
God is Spirit, and those who worship Him must worship in spirit and truth.

John 6:63
It is the Spirit who gives life; the flesh profits nothing. The words that I speak to you are spirit, and they are life.

John 15:4-5
Abide in Me, and I in you. As the branch cannot bear fruit of itself, unless it abides in the vine, neither can you, unless you abide in Me. I am the vine, you are the branches. He who abides in Me, and I in him, bears much fruit; for without Me you can do nothing.

Romans 1:9

For God is my witness, whom I serve with my spirit in the gospel of His Son, that without ceasing I make mention of you always in my prayers,

Romans 5:17

For if by the one man's offense death reigned through the one, much more those who receive abundance of grace and of the gift of righteousness will reign in life through the One, Jesus Christ.

Romans 8:1-2

There is therefore now no condemnation to those who are in Christ Jesus, who do not walk according to the flesh, but according to the Spirit. For the law of the Spirit of life in Christ Jesus has made me free from the law of sin and death.

Romans 6:12-13

Therefore do not let sin reign in your mortal body, that you should obey it in its lusts. And do not present your members as instruments of unrighteousness to sin, but present yourselves to God as being alive from the dead, and your members as instruments of righteousness to God.

THE REAL YOU

Romans 8:5
For those who live according to the flesh set their minds on the things of the flesh, but those who live according to the Spirit, the things of the Spirit.

Romans 8:11
But if the Spirit of Him who raised Jesus from the dead dwells in you, He who raised Christ from the dead will also give life to your mortal bodies through His Spirit who dwells in you.

Romans 8:12-13
Therefore, brethren, we are debtors—not to the flesh, to live according to the flesh. For if you live according to the flesh you will die; but if by the Spirit you put to death the deeds of the body, you will live.

Romans 8:14-17
For as many as are led by the Spirit of God, these are sons of God. For you did not receive the spirit of bondage again to fear, but you received the Spirit of adoption by whom we cry out, "Abba, Father." The Spirit Himself bears witness with our spirit that we are children of God.

Romans 12:1-2
I beseech you therefore, brethren, by the mercies of God,

that you present your bodies a living sacrifice, holy, acceptable to God, which is your reasonable service. And do not be conformed to this world, but be transformed by the renewing of your mind, that you may prove what is that good and acceptable and perfect will of God.

1 Corinthians 6:19-20

Or do you not know that your body is the temple of the Holy Spirit who is in you, whom you have from God, and you are not your own? For you were bought at a price; therefore glorify God in your body and in your spirit, which are God's.

1 Corinthians 9:27

But I discipline my body and bring it into subjection, lest, when I have preached to others, I myself should become disqualified.

1 Corinthians 13:4-8

Love suffers long and is kind; love does not envy; love does not parade itself, is not puffed up; does not behave rudely, does not seek its own, is not provoked, thinks no evil; does not rejoice in iniquity, but rejoices in the truth; bears all things, believes all things, hopes all things, endures all things. Love never fails. But whether there are prophecies, they will fail; whether there are tongues, they will cease;

THE REAL YOU

whether there is knowledge, it will vanish away.

1 Corinthians 14:14
For if I pray in a tongue, my spirit prays, but my understanding is unfruitful.

2 Corinthians 4:16-18
Therefore we do not lose heart. Even though our outward man is perishing, yet the inward man is being renewed day by day. For our light affliction, which is but for a moment, is working for us a far more exceeding and eternal weight of glory, while we do not look at the things which are seen, but at the things which are not seen. For the things which are seen are temporary, but the things which are not seen are eternal.

2 Corinthians 5:6-8
So we are always confident, knowing that while we are at home in the body we are absent from the Lord. For we walk by faith, not by sight. We are confident, yes, well pleased rather to be absent from the body and to be present with the Lord.

2 Corinthians 5:16-17
Therefore, from now on, we regard no one according to

the flesh. Even though we have known Christ according to the flesh, yet now we know Him thus no longer. Therefore, if anyone is in Christ, he is a new creation; old things have passed away; behold, all things have become new.

2 Corinthians 10:4-5
For the weapons of our warfare are not carnal but mighty in God for pulling down strongholds, casting down arguments and every high thing that exalts itself against the knowledge of God, bringing every thought into captivity to the obedience of Christ,

Galatians 5:16
I say then: Walk in the Spirit, and you shall not fulfill the lust of the flesh.

Galatians 5:22-23
But the fruit of the Spirit is love, joy, peace, longsuffering, kindness, goodness, faithfulness, gentleness, self-control. Against such there is no law.

Ephesians 2:10 (AMP)
For we are God's [own] handiwork (His workmanship), recreated in Christ Jesus, [born anew] that we may do those good works which God predestined (planned be-

THE REAL YOU

forehand) for us [taking paths which He prepared ahead of time], that we should walk in them [living the good life which He prearranged and made ready for us to live].

Ephesians 4:24
And that you put on the new man which was created according to God, in true righteousness and holiness.

Colossians 3:1-2
If then you were raised with Christ, seek those things which are above, where Christ is, sitting at the right hand of God. **Set your mind on things above**, not on things on the earth. For you died, and your life is hidden with Christ in God.

1 Thessalonians 5:23
Now may the God of peace Himself sanctify you completely; and may your whole spirit, soul, and body be preserved blameless at the coming of our Lord Jesus Christ.

Hebrews 4:12
For the word of God is living and powerful, and sharper than any two-edged sword, piercing even to the division of soul and spirit, and of joints and marrow, and is a discerner of the thoughts and intents of the heart.

Hebrews 5:13-14

For everyone who partakes only of milk is unskilled in the word of righteousness, for he is a babe. But solid food belongs to those who are of full age, that is, those who by reason of use have their senses exercised to discern both good and evil.

Hebrews 9:12-14

Not with the blood of goats and calves, but with His own blood He entered the Most Holy Place once for all, having obtained eternal redemption. For if the blood of bulls and goats and the ashes of a heifer, sprinkling the unclean, sanctifies for the purifying of the flesh, how much more shall the blood of Christ, who through the eternal Spirit offered Himself without spot to God, cleanse your conscience from dead works to serve the living God?

James 1:21

Therefore lay aside all filthiness and overflow of wickedness, and receive with meekness the implanted word, which is able to save your souls.

James 1:22-25

But be doers of the word, and not hearers only, deceiving yourselves. For if anyone is a hearer of the word and not a doer, he is like a man observing his natural face in a mirror; for he observes himself, goes away, and immediately forgets what kind of man he was. But he who looks into the perfect law of liberty and continues in it, and is not a forgetful hearer but a doer of the work, this one will be blessed in what he does.

James 2:26
For as the body without the spirit is dead, so faith without works is dead also.

1 Peter 1:4
to an inheritance incorruptible and undefiled and that does not fade away, reserved in heaven for you

1 Peter 1:23
having been born again, not of corruptible seed but incorruptible, through the word of God which lives and abides forever,

1 Peter 4:19
Therefore let those who suffer according to the will of God commit their souls to Him in doing good, as to a faithful Creator.

NOTES

NOTES

NOTES

NOTES

NOTES

NOTES

HOW TO BE BORN AGAIN

The way to get *in Christ* is to be born again. Jesus said that it is a person's spirit that must be born again. This miracle, by the Holy Spirit, will happen within you the moment you call on Jesus to be your personal Lord and Savior. God is now offering you a new life, and an eternal home in Heaven with Him. It's as simple as A, B, C:

Acknowledge that you are a sinner, separated from God, and in need of salvation.
For all have sinned and fall short of the glory of God. (Romans 3:23)

Believe that Jesus Christ, the Son of God, died for your sins and rose again from the dead.
But God demonstrates His own love toward us, in that while we were still sinners, Christ died for us. (Romans 5:8)

Confess (say) with your mouth, "Jesus is Lord!"
That if you confess with your mouth the Lord Jesus and believe in your heart that God has raised him from the dead, you will be saved. (Romans 10:9)

To receive Jesus as your Lord and Savior simply pray this prayer:

> **God in heaven, I turn from sin to You. I believe in my heart that Jesus died for my sin and rose again. Jesus, come into my life and be my Lord. Thank You for saving me. Today, I am born again! Amen.**

If you prayed the prayer to receive Jesus Christ as your Lord and Savior, please contact us on the web at www.wordoflifelv.com, by email, info@wordoflifelv.com, call us at (702) 645-1990 ext. 101 or write us at: Word of Life Christian Center, 3520 N. Buffalo Dr., Las Vegas, Nevada 89129.

ACKNOWLEDGEMENTS

I would like to acknowledge with deepest gratitude…

My wife Vicki and daughter Ashley who have sacrificed greatly for me to be able to fulfill the call of God upon my life.

My mother Lannie Shearin, now in heaven whose prayers and godly example have given me stability in every season of my life.

My spiritual fathers, Reverend Kenneth E. ("Dad") Hagin and Pastor B.B. Hankins, who are cheering me on from the grandstands of heaven.

My pastors for nearly forty years, Phil and Barbara Privette.

Mark and Trina Hankins, who have been true friends and spiritual mentors to Vicki and me for more than thirty years.

My staff, whose assistance and support was so vital in the writing of *The Real You, Unveiling the Hidden Person of the Heart*.

Experience David Shearin's audio or video messages
The Real You, *Unveiling the Hidden Person of the Heart*
CD and DVD series

Other Books By David Shearin:
The Master Key: Unlock the Mystery of Supernatural Living
Tapping Into Wisdom's Treasures

To order products by David and Vicki Shearin
visit us on the web
@ www.thewordforliving.com or call (866) 700-9673

TELEVISION BROADCAST:
The Word For Living
Check the website for listings at www.thewordforliving.com

CHURCH SERVICES:
Word of Life Christian Center
Sundays @ 8:00am, 10:30am & 6:30pm Wednesdays @ 7:00pm
3520 N. Buffalo Dr. • Las Vegas, NV 89129

Phone: (702) 645-1990 • Fax: (702) 645-3641

E-mail: info@wordoflifelasvegas.com
Visit us on the web @ **www.wordoflifelv.com**
or **www.thewordforliving.com**

ALSO AVAILABLE BY PASTOR DAVID SHEARIN...

THE MASTER KEY

Deep within our spirit, we can all sense that we have a divine destiny. The desire for it burns in our hearts like an eternal flame. As we try to move forward into the abundant life Jesus promised us in the Bible we often fall short, and it sometimes seems as if the door to it is locked.

It's a puzzle. We know this isn't God's will for us. We know it isn't our destiny. But the solution is a mystery!

This book is about a key that unlocks this mystery—the Master Key revealed in the New Testament again and again through the words "in Christ". Whether you've been a Christian for days or for decades, your life will be enriched as you deepen your understanding of the mystery of being in Christ.

Tapping Into Wisdom's Treasures

Do you often find yourself in pressure situations where you feel like you don't have the wisdom to make the right decisions? Pressure often pushes people into making poor choices. God's wisdom will keep pressure from pushing you around. Tapping Into Wisdom's Treasures will teach you how to listen to God and draw wisdom from The Holy Spirit. He'll give you His insight and prudence so you will know what to do, when to do it, how to do it, and with whom to do it, and the blessing of God will be on your life!

ORDER ONLINE AT
WWW.THEWORDFORLIVING.COM

"A moral and spiritual snapshot of America and what we must do... Wake up America!"
– John Hagee

NEW RELEASE! FROM VICKI SHEARIN

Vicki Shearin sounds an alarm of warning to the church in America after being awakened by the voice of God. "Sodom or Salem?" is the question Vicki heard that literally woke her up after falling asleep one night. Sodom represents judgment and Salem is the earliest name for Jerusalem, which means peace. With compelling historical evidence and Scriptural revelation, Vicki explains how "We the People" can avoid Sodom, choose Salem, and turn America back to the founding principles that made her the greatest nation on earth!

Available at
amazon

Download a free sample chapter at
www.wordoflifelv.com/sodomorsalem

About The Author

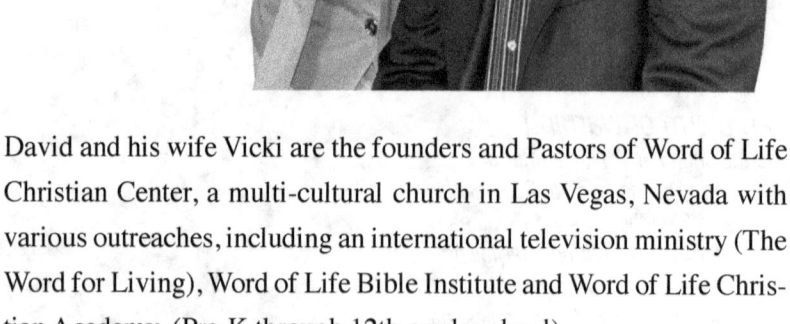

David and his wife Vicki are the founders and Pastors of Word of Life Christian Center, a multi-cultural church in Las Vegas, Nevada with various outreaches, including an international television ministry (The Word for Living), Word of Life Bible Institute and Word of Life Christian Academy, (Pre-K through 12th grade school).

Pastor David Shearin, a man of integrity and compassion, is a dynamic preacher and teacher of God's Word. He and his wife Vicki, both minister with boldness, humor, and compassion. In addition to pastoring, they are frequent speakers for conferences across the U.S. and overseas. Both are graduates of Rhema Bible Training College and have been in full-time ministry for 34 years. They have one daughter, Ashley, who works with them in ministry.

David is the author of three books, ***The Master Key: Unlock the Mystery of Supernatural Living, Tapping Into Wisdom's Treasures,*** and his latest book, ***The Real You: Unveiling the Hidden Person of the Heart.*** Vicki recently authored the book, ***Sodom or Salem? America it's Your Choice.***

www.ingramcontent.com/pod-product-compliance
Lightning Source LLC
Chambersburg PA
CBHW070054120526
44588CB00033B/1430